THE ART OF BECOMING

QUANTUM LEAPING INTO YOUR FUTURE SELF

COREY LEE LEWIS, PH.D.

BALBOA.
PRESS

A DIVISION OF HAY HOUSE

Balboa Press books may be ordered through booksellers or by contacting:

Balboa Press
A Division of Hay House
1663 Liberty Drive
Bloomington, IN 47403
www.balboapress.com
1 (877) 407-4847

Because of the dynamic nature of the Internet, any web addresses or links contained in this book may have changed since publication and may no longer be valid. The views expressed in this work are solely those of the author and do not necessarily reflect the views of the publisher, and the publisher hereby disclaims any responsibility for them.

The author of this book does not dispense medical advice or prescribe the use of any technique as a form of treatment for physical, emotional, or medical problems without the advice of a physician, either directly or indirectly. The intent of the author is only to offer information of a general nature to help you in your quest for emotional and spiritual well-being. In the event you use any of the information in this book for yourself, which is your constitutional right, the author and the publisher assume no responsibility for your actions.

Any people depicted in stock imagery provided by Thinkstock are models, and such images are being used for illustrative purposes only. Certain stock imagery © Thinkstock.

Print information available on the last page.

ISBN: 978-1-5043-5956-6 (sc)
ISBN: 978-1-5043-5957-3 (hc)
ISBN: 978-1-5043-5973-3 (e)

Library of Congress Control Number: 2016909220

Balboa Press rev. date: 07/11/2016

To Mom and Dad

Because you believed in me
and all of my big dreams
Because you taught me, through both word and deed,
the power of love, enthusiasm and effort
and most importantly
Because you showed me
you have to give to receive

CONTENTS

ACKNOWLEDGEMENTS

I have been blessed with many teachers over the years.
It is nearly impossible to list them all, but you know who you are.
Not only have each of you made my life better and richer,
You have also made the lives of those I have
touched, change for the better.
Your impact continues to ripple out in waves across
countless lives over the entire multi-verse.

Warning

A Disclaimer to All Readers
As a Doctor I am advised to warn you of the
serious side effects of reading this book.
Do not read this book if...
You do not want to Be who you have always
known you should Become.
You do not want your wildest dreams to be
a living part of your daily reality.
You do not want to be happier, more fulfilled
and more effective than ever.
You do not want to give copies of this book to
friends to help their dreams come true.

THE BEGINNING

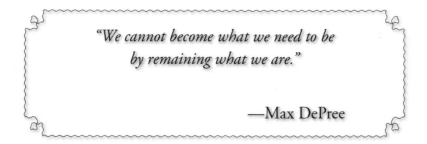

> *"We cannot become what we need to be*
> *by remaining what we are."*
>
> —Max DePree

What if you could jump into a parallel universe and experience an alternate self, live a different life?

Or what if you could travel through time, go to your future and return with things that would improve and enrich your present?

What if you could leap over the breakdowns and tough times in your life, to the breakthroughs and bright future on the other side?

If there was a way to bring your future into your present, to Be Now who and what you dream of Becoming, how badly would you want to learn it?

I can teach you how to do that and even more.

I wrote this book as a road map to show you, my readers, exactly how to do what I have already done.

My journeys into the future began out of a need to meet my future self and train under my own tutelage. They began because I was a wreck emotionally. Devastated by divorce and the deaths of two loved ones, I desperately needed to heal.

There are times when life sends you reeling, like a punch drunk fighter who has just taken one on the chin, head spinning, lost in a daze, you stagger around not knowing what to do or even where you are. That's how I felt when I turned forty.

My wife had just left me and I was broken-hearted on so many levels that it's hard to capture the hurt, loss and loneliness in words. Of course, as unique, specific and special as our own heartbreak feels, everyone who has loved and lost has felt that same heart-wrenching, crushing feeling.

In many ways, it felt like I had lost my entire life not just my wife. We were happily married with two boys. In fact, I grew up in a loving and wonderful family with one brother and had always wanted to have the exact same thing when I grew up. So losing my marriage and family felt like I was losing my entire life, losing everything I had longed for, wanted and worked for since I was a kid.

I watched myself as if I were moving through life in a daze and knew that something had to change. I knew that there had to be more, that I had an important purpose to fulfill, but I had no idea how to discover what it was.

So I began training with him—with my future self—because there simply was no one else in the world who could point me to all the right teachers and teach me everything I needed to learn in order to heal my wounds and find my true purpose. It was time to step into who I knew I was supposed to be, time to regain what I had lost and time to discover what I was supposed to give others.

I was ready to learn it all, to manifest the latent skills inside me that I was meant to, and the only person who knew those skills and the path toward attaining them lived in the future. The only person who could teach the middle-aged me was the elderly me, the one who had already lived through those decades of life and learning, the one who had already met those teachers, read those books and lived through those experiences.

And the same thing holds true for you, right now. Your greatest present teacher is your future self.

So I began astral projecting, or quantum leaping forward into my own future on this plane of existence in order to meet and learn from my future self through meditation. These quantum leaps and our conversations began quite simply in an armchair in my own home, but they didn't end there. In fact, they never ended at all. They took me and continue to take me, all over the multi-verse—to the past, present and several potential futures.

Perhaps I should describe the experience for you first, tell you what a quantum leap feels like and then I can tell you about the science and theory behind the process.

As I left my meditating body I would feel myself propelled up into the sky, flying forward and upward toward the clouds. I had been taking flying lessons for several months at the time that I started quantum leaping so I had good clear images in my memory to work with.

I would fly higher and higher, like going up for a power-on stall with the stall siren wailing, but during this flight all was quiet. Silently

I sailed up and through the clouds and into the bright expanse of sky and space. Far out ahead of me I could see the vast blackness of space filled with bright blinking stars and swirling lights and colors.

Then I felt my momentum slow and my body turn, and at the zenith of my arc, I stood before a door. Opening it and stepping through, I suddenly felt myself falling down the back side of the arc, just like cresting that first hill on a roller coaster. I would drop down through a swirling black tube, with colors and darkness spinning around me while sounds buzzed in my head, until I was spit out into the bright emptiness of space again.

Then I would feel a second drop and I was falling back down through clouds and plummeting toward the earth. I watched as the planet rushed up to meet me, seeing greens and browns coming into view, then mountains and forests and open meadows, until I recognized my parents' place in the Colorado Rockies. This is where Corey would usually choose to meet me for our conversations. I could see their house below, rushing up toward me.

My momentum would slow as I neared the ground and I'd drop softly into a chair on the deck. Then, unhurried and as natural as you please, Corey would emerge from the house, usually with two cups of tea in his hands and we would begin to talk.

The idea to begin quantum jumping or leaping into my future came to me from my Silva Method training. Jose Silva is world famous for his Silva Mind Control Method which essentially teaches you how to reach Alpha brain wave levels and do powerfully transformative work there with your conscious and unconscious mind.

In our waking state, Beta, our brains produce waves at about 21 cycles per second. As we relax into a meditative trance or hypnotic state, our brain waves slow to Alpha, which is between 7 and 14 cycles per second. Below that is Delta, sleep, and farther down is Theta, unconsciousness. Once we enter the Alpha state we can program the unconscious directly, both hemispheres of our brain are activated and MRIs show a larger percentage of our brain is being used than at any other time and thus we have a wide range of new perceptions and abilities in this state.

Burt Goldman, a long time Silva Method instructor and practitioner, initially developed the concept and practice of quantum jumping. The basic concept comes out of Quantum Physics: that there are an infinite number of alternate planes of existence, that we live in a multi-verse and that it is theoretically possible to bridge time-space and visit these other planes of existence in the multi-verse.

In each alternate plane of existence, we have an alternate self, who has made different choices and lived different lives. These selves have come to be called doppelgangers, "twin walkers."

Burt decided while teaching a course on creativity, to go to Alpha level and leap to one of these parallel realities where his doppelganger was a famous photographer. After several meditation sessions or quantum leaps, Burt who had no training in photography created a technique, now called "Burtons," of taking hundreds of photos from one location and putting them together like a puzzle to create a single photo. He later used quantum jumping to become a pianist, and yet he cannot read music and doesn't know chords, but plays beautifully. Similarly, although he had never painted before he used quantum leaping to become a sought after artist, whose work sells well and now hangs in museums all over the world... The list goes on, with a variety of newly acquired talents and skills that usually take a life-time to master. And Burt did it all after the age of 70.

If there were no limits put upon you, what skills would you like to have? Who would you like to be?

In your wildest imagination and daydreams what life have you dreamed of that you have not yet lived?

Where is that one place in the world you have always wanted to go or that one thing you have always wanted to do?

What are those things and experiences that you want your future to be filled with but don't know how to get?

Like most adults I know, I was carrying around the weight of life's ordinary but devastating losses and I wanted something more out of life to be happy, but I wasn't sure what that was. After college and graduate school and tenure I was a success. I had arrived. But there was this nagging feeling, this troubling thought like a splinter in the mind that kept saying "you are supposed to do more, be more." But, I did not yet know what that was or how to become it.

That we can find our answers within ourselves, through reflection and meditation is not a new concept. Nor is the idea that we can find our answers outside ourselves, through prayer, observation and invocation. It did however, strike me as a new thought that our answers could be found by doing both at the same time, that going inside was the same as going outside.

But these kinds of paradoxes I would soon learn are common in Quantum Physics. The farther I got into studying the field the more I got the feeling of going down the rabbit hole like I was reading science fiction instead of science.

In fact, Niels Bohr, one of the field's foremost founders and experts famously wrote: "If Quantum Mechanics hasn't profoundly shocked you, you haven't understood it yet."

One shocker that the Nobel Prize winner discovered was that once subatomic particles come into contact with each other, they forever after influence each other, instantaneously, over any time and distance. This effect is called "Entanglement" or "Non-Locality," referring to the inter-connected or entangled nature of the particles, and the fact that location or the space separating them has no impact on their ability to affect each other or the time it takes for that effect to cover the distance between them. Once two particles are entangled the actions of one will always and instantaneously, influence the other, no matter how far they are separated.

Understanding how entanglement works helps us to understand how quantum leaping to your future self can change you in the here and now. If you get on the same wave-length with, if you get entangled with that future self, then it will influence you and you will influence it.

This selective process is called "personal resonance" and can be compared to a vibrating tuning fork which will only create resonance with another tuning fork if they are similar in size, shape and structure. Thus, theoretically, by tuning into our own personal resonance and using Alpha level meditation, we can get on the same frequency as one of our doppelgangers in another space or time and merge with or become entangled with it.

Once we have become entangled on the quantum level we will, like the subatomic quanta we are made of, influence and be influenced by those we are entangled with "instantaneously." Therefore, it appeared clear to me that if I could become entangled with my future self, when I returned to the present from meditation I would not only have absorbed some of his frequency, but would maintain a direct connection to him and continue to be influenced by him.

What better way to become who I want to be, I thought, then to have him influence me directly and energetically on the sub-atomic level?

Let me give one simple but powerful example of the power of resonant frequency in our ordinary, physical world and common experience. Have you ever heard of an opera singer shattering glass with her voice? How is this possible? Without any impact, without hitting or striking or dropping the glass, how does she transfer so much energy into it that the glass shatters, instantly into hundreds of pieces?

If the glass was matter and her voice was energy (as many of us perceive them to be) then it would be impossible for her to break the glass. However since the glass itself is energy, waves vibrating at a particular resonant frequency, when she tunes the frequency of her voice into that same resonance, into that same channel, then she can add the energy of her voice to that wave's frequency, changing its resonant vibration so much that it can no longer hold itself together in solid form.

When we energetically link up with our other self, when we match his or her frequency and focus on it, then we can pull that vibration into our reality with us. And we will be able to manifest in physical form the material match to that energetic vibration or frequency.

Burt Goldman explains this in musical terms, noting that since all things are surrounded and infused by their own energy field, vibrating at their own specific frequency, we can think of this as an octave. On some octaves the frequency is faster or slower, thus all things have their own vibrational rhythm. People who are successful for example, have a different rhythm or frequency than those who are not.

You cannot bring back the material things you see in other realities, but through quantum leaping you can bring back their specific rhythm, their particular frequency and use it here, until material reality matches it.

Similarly, since we live in a space-time system, it is theoretically possible to leap in time, just as it is to leap in space. In fact, non-locality applies to time in precisely the same way that it applies to space. Every time, every past, present and possible future, can be understood to be happening at once, to exist at the same moment.

This amazing characteristic of the multi-verse to contain all times and spaces is best understood through learning how holographic film works and how holograms are created. When you shine a light through holographic film, whatever is recorded on it will appear in a three-dimensional hologram, an image that can be viewed from any angle. Remember *Star Wars*, if you will, and R2D2 playing the holographic video of Princess Leah asking for OB-Wan Kenobi's help.

One of the most fascinating things about holograms is that if you cut the holographic film in half, you don't get half the image like you would with any regular film. You still get the entire image just not as bright. Even if you cut the film into a hundred pieces and use only the smallest piece, you still get an entire image because the information for the entire image is not recorded in one place on the film, it is recorded everywhere.

As Michael Talbot explains in *The Holographic Universe*, this is precisely the nature of our multi-verse and space-time. Since the information for everything is stored everywhere in the holographic universe other space-times are accessible in the here-now.

Theories like these from Quantum Physics, plus years of meditating and having outer body experiences, along with hearing about Burt Goldman's technique gave me the idea of quantum leaping to my own future, to meet with and learn from myself.

I knew that at some point in my future I would be happy and healthy again. I knew that eventually I would heal, overcome my loss and discover my life's purpose. But I couldn't see how to get there from here—from where I was at the time.

"If Burt can jump to alternate planes of existence and learn from himself, why can't I leap to a future time on this plane of existence and learn from myself?" I thought.

And so I did.

When I sat down to do my first leap, I can still recall that there was no question in my mind whether or not it would work. I knew I would be able to meet Corey and to see him and talk to him. I did wonder a little bit however, if what he would tell me would be immediately useful and clearly understandable or completely confusing and mystically abstract. I should have known, since he was me that I would get both, that I would get exactly what I wanted and more.

I should have known that I was in for a loving ass kicking!

I sat back in my office chair and began to draw deep breaths in and deep breaths out. I talked myself down, relaxing, dropping deeper and further still into Alpha brain wave levels, until I settled into that comfortable and familiar meditative state.

Then I imagined myself floating up above my body and out through the roof of the house and on up into the sky. As I glanced back I saw a silver thread connecting me to my body which sat reclining comfortably in my office chair. As I continued to soar skyward I sailed through clouds and then out into bright sky and so much space surrounding me on all sides that the earth was just a small ball below.

And then as my momentum slowed, almost to a stop, my arc flattened out and I felt myself go over the crest, step through the doorway, and begin falling. As I flew downward, I gained momentum, falling faster and faster, until I could see the green fields and forests and gray peaks of the Rockies zooming up toward me.

On that first leap, my momentum slowed just in time and I found myself plopped down in a chair on the deck of my parent's house in Colorado. Even before he came out of the house, carrying what I would soon recognize as his customary cups of tea, I realized Corey had already given me some very clear information. The location of our meeting itself told me that I was going to end up living, at least for a good portion of the year, in this house in Colorado, instead of (or in addition to) California where I lived at the time.

"So I'll be moving." I thought.

And then he came outside. It was strangely familiar or strangely not strange at all to see him, like looking in the mirror or at an old photograph of yourself from when you were a kid. You recognize yourself and register the differences: a bit more salt and pepper in the hair, more laugh lines, brighter eyes, same voice, sharper mind…

"Well C," he said, as he sat down across from me. "So we begin…" During our conversations he always called me "C" while I referred to him as "Corey," because, as he explained "You aren't me yet, pal. You aren't fully yourself yet, so I will call you "C" until you are Being who you are supposed to Become."

He held up his cup and we toasted. "So what have you come here for? What do you want to get out of this?"

"Damn he's direct." I thought. "But then what did I expect? I mean, I'm pretty direct and he's just more me…"

"HA!" Corey barked in a short ki-yap-like way, interrupting my train of thoughts. "You might want to just cut all that internal dialogue shit out and focus or we won't get anywhere." Corey said with a laugh and a wink. "I know what you're thinking anyway"

"Okay, so what do I want? Well, you really want to know?" I asked and then it all came flooding out. "I want to stop crying. I want this hole in my chest to go away. I want to stop running resentments and regrets through my head. I want to stop feeling broken, fragile and like a failure. I want you to show me how to be you, how to be who I am supposed to become. I want you to teach me what I need to learn and what I need to do and how to be happy."

"And why do you want those things C?"

"Because I'm tired of being mad and sad and feeling broken and lost. Because I miss my wife and wish I wasn't divorced and I miss my brother and wish he wouldn't have died and I wish my best friend Tim was still alive because I miss him too and I don't know how to go on and I know I have big important things to give and do, but I don't know what or how."

"So in a word C, what you want is to-- CHANGE!" Corey paused right before saying the last word and then, when he said it, he yelled it abruptly, sharply like a command, his voice dropping down at the end of the word. I felt a shock run through my entire nervous system, a shock that I would later learn was a sign that he was already reprogramming me on a neurological level with our conversation.

"Yes, I want to change, to change everything." I replied, the tears streaming down my cheeks.

"No, you want to CHANGE YOURSELF, NOW you are going to learn how to do that and then you will teach it to others, how to heal themselves, how to optimize themselves, how to know what their purpose is and how to fulfill it."

"The first thing I'm going to teach you about is *The Universal Law of Change*. You might even call it *The Universal Law of Growth*. The only constant is change C. Everything changes all the time. Change is growth. Growth is change."

"What do you know about the Universe C?"

"Well, that it started as a big bang a long, long time ago, and it's infinite and ever-expanding outward and…"

"Exactly!" He cut me off. "Ever-Expanding. What does that mean?"

"I guess it means constantly changing." I replied.

"Precisely C. If we like the change we call it growth or evolution. If we don't like it we call it regression or decay. But it's all the same. It's still just change. You are either growing or dying, evolving or decaying and you are always changing."

"Now the question is, do you want to change by growing and evolving or change by decaying and dying? Because you know, although change is inevitable, growth is optional."

"I want to grow, of course." I replied.

"Really, are you sure?" He was questioning me, baiting me, and it pissed me off.

"You are damned right I'm sure! I've never wanted anything more!"

"Good, that's a good place to start, because you better be committed and I mean fully committed to changing. You have got to know that change is brutal in the beginning, messy in the middle and exquisite in the end. And you've got to know that it's coming. Change is here...Change is now..."

As he spoke we were transported to somewhere that was more a space than a place. It was dark, and felt like a combination of all the locker rooms and pre-fight prep rooms I had spent so many years in as a competitive martial artist. It had that same feel, but it didn't look like any particular locker room I remember. I could feel his voice behind me, his hands on my back and shoulders, the familiar pre-fight rub down. I could feel myself moving, that familiar pre-fight jogging in place and swaying—it has a pacing feel to it, like you are a caged tiger.

As he spoke, his voice rose in volume and pitch. I could feel the energy rising, surging and spinning in my body.

"If you want to change you have got to want it. You have got to want to change more than anything. You've got to want it more than you want to breathe."

"You've got to give up some shit to do it too. You have to be willing at each and every moment to sacrifice who you are today for who you will become. You have got to drop your resentments and let go of your losses and put away your pains. You have to be willing to turn your pain into power, to turn your losses into learnings, and your tragedies into triumphs."

"You have to get up, not give up, from your fall. You've got to know that your challenges will either make you bitter or better; It's up to you, so you have got to steel yourself for the effort ahead. You have to make the decision and the commitment now that no matter how hard it gets, no matter how much pain you are in, you will keep going. You have got to push through pain and fight through fatigue. Because if you stop, the pain will last forever."

"You've got to know it's not about where you come from, it's about where you are going.

"You've got to know it's possible and you've got to believe to achieve. You've got to believe when others doubt and persevere when others quit, in order to succeed where others fail."

"You got to get certain about your success. You have got to say 'I can do this! I will do this! I am doing this!'"

At this point Corey was yelling in my ear and I was sweating and covered with goose-bumps, so jacked on adrenaline and powerful emotions that every cell felt like it was electrified.

Then, he whispered in my ear and shoved me forward into the light. "Go get to work champ."

I was blinded by the stadium lights, but could hear the deafening roar of the crowd and then suddenly, I was sitting in my desk chair at home. The bright white light of a blank document washed over me from the open computer screen and a chainsaw growled across the mountain gorge. The cursor blinked invitingly and I began to write:

The Art of Becoming
Quantum Leaping into Your Future Self

Chapter One
The Beginning

What if you could jump into a parallel universe and …

CHAPTER TWO

EVERYTHING IS A GIFT

*"When we are no longer able to
change a situation –
We are challenged to change ourselves."*

—Viktor Frankl

Many people have noticed that troubles, the difficulties in our lives, often come in packs. They seem to come in sets, in waves, where we are beset by several different challenges all at once. And so we get the familiar saying, "it never rains, but it pours," troubles don't come a little at a time they tend to come flooding down all at once.

Often when we experience this, it is merely a matter of perception. We suffer one trouble and it colors our perception, distorts it, and has us seeing difficulties and problems everywhere. In such times, believing is seeing. It is important not to focus too much on our troubles, on our defeats, mistakes and failures, because they can cloud our vision, and over-take our entire outlook on the world, until problems are all we can see everywhere.

But sometimes, it really is the case that we are confronted with a number of life-altering difficulties all at once. Most often, in fact, before people experience monumental periods of growth and success, they have a period of intense hardship and difficulty. Most often there is a breakdown before there can be a breakthrough. This was exactly the case for me. In the span of two years I lost my only brother to cancer, my best friend to a drug overdose, and my wife to divorce.

I lost three of the most important people in my life. I was devastated.

I was Lost.

Overwhelmed.

My older brother and I were always very close and at the time he died we were talking on the phone every single day. He was battling cancer and remodeling homes; we both had young families and I was remodeling a warehouse to turn it into my Tae Kwon Do school, so I would call him daily with some question about construction. These calls would invariably end with him saying "do you have time for a joke?" and then he would regale me with a bawdy joke that I had never even heard before. I don't know where he got them all, some surely came from his daily AA meetings, but still his repertoire was amazing and it never seemed to end.

We were always the closest of brothers. In fact, my parents like to tell how on the way home from the hospital when I was born, Bart demanded from the backseat "Hurry home, I want to hold my baby brother." And hold me he did, all of our lives growing up: he taught me how to read, about sports and girls and about life.

Bart struggled with drug and alcohol addiction for most of his adult life. He was a chronic relapser, and would work hard and do well at getting his life back together, making good grades or getting a good job, only to see all of that disappear after a relapse would send him spiraling down for weeks until he was penniless, homeless and on the street. Eventually, he beat his addiction, became a drug and alcohol counselor and helped others to turn their own lives around.

In the end, when he died of cancer at the age of forty, he was truly an enlightened man. He had endured more hardships and suffered more than most people could handle. From child abuse, to living on the streets as a crack addict, to being jailed and beaten, being struck by lightning, surviving car wrecks, losing friends and loved ones, facing suicide, and finally contracting cancer, Bart had more bad things happen to him than any single person deserves, or could even imagine.

And despite all of these hardships, or perhaps because of them, Bart used to say to me "Everything that happens in life, Corey, is a gift." Then he would get an intense look in his eyes and he would say, in that special way that was uniquely his, where he would add an "x" to the word especially, he would say "Everything is a gift Corey, ex-specially the bad stuff. Your job is to figure out what that gift is and to give it back to the universe."

And you could ask Bart about anything that happened in his life, about any of those dark times, those tragedies and that suffering, and for each and every one, he could tell you what the gift was. And you could see by the way he lived his life that he was giving that gift back to the world.

In fact this is precisely what he did on the night that he died. He called to tell me he was dying and most likely wouldn't make it through the night and he said "Although I don't want to die Corey, and leave my girls behind…" He always called his wife and two daughters "his girls." "I've accepted it. And that's part of the gift Corey. I've accepted it and you have to also."

"I want you to remember this Corey," he said, and other than "I love you" it was the last thing he ever said to me, "Everything is a gift."

"What Bart was teaching you about C," Corey explained to me, "is another *Universal Law* called *The Law of Perception*. Simply put this law states that your perceptions create your reality, that believing is seeing. It shows us that the meaning we attribute to any event, whether we define it as good or bad, is completely arbitrary or relative, completely dependent upon how we perceive it, dependent upon the point of view from which we see it."

"How you choose to perceive your divorce and Bart and Tim's passing will dictate how you experience them."

"Yeah but Corey, there's no way I can see them as something good."

"Not yet C," Corey replied in a haunting whisper, "But, you will."

"Do you recall C, that Archimedes famously said 'Give me a lever and a place to stand and I shall move the world?' What's most important here is not the lever, but the place to stand—not the tool we are using, but our standpoint—where we are viewing things from. From our human perspective, it's terrible your brother and your best friend died. From a soul's point of view, from the perspective of a spirit incarnating into and out of physical form, it's a joyous return home to complete bliss and just one of many experiences in an infinite, ongoing process."

Intellectually I could understand what Corey was saying, but it was hard to feel it—to believe it, especially with the way that my losses seemed to be compounding. Not long after losing Bart, I lost my wife and my entire sense of purpose, as the family we had built together seemed to be torn asunder. I had been married for 10 years to a beautiful woman, who I absolutely adored. Then suddenly it seemed like my entire world came crashing down in divorce. We had two wonderful boys, a family life with camping trips, fun in the home, lots of love and joy: everything that I had dreamed of and wanted my entire life, everything I had as a child and wanted to re-create as an adult. I identified completely as a husband, father and family man. And when we split, I felt like a major part of me, many parts of me had died.

I was hurt. I felt broken inside. Life seemed to lose its meaning. It was hard to even think about going on, how to go on and even why to go on.

I had watched friends suffer from divorces, many of them spiraling downward for a year or two after their divorce, before they began to heal and claw their way back up to normalcy once again. I vowed not to lose two years of my life, or even two months, to depression, suffering, wallowing in pity and pain.

But despite this decision I knew how they felt. I understood how it felt to lose your best friend and your lover and your family and yourself. It felt like I had lost all four of these things, like I had lost not only a part of myself, but everything I had worked for and everything that I cared about in life.

Then my best friend from High School died of an accidental OxyContin overdose. We were such good friends that in the time since High School we had been roommates in college, lived together in several different states, traveled together in a number of countries and worked together professionally on a number of businesses. After his divorce in fact, Tim moved from where he was living at the time in Reno, to Arcata to live in an apartment in my Tae Kwon

Do school and help me remodel it and open it for business. So at the time of my divorce, he was my closest friend and confidant, the pillar of support that was going to help me get through it, just as I had helped him get through his divorce. And then just like that, the Doctors and pharmaceutical companies with their deadly and addictive prescriptions, snatched him away in his sleep and my best friend was gone.

With Tim gone too, I felt completely alone, like a ship far out at sea without sail or rudder.

I knew I needed some technique, some way to help me shift out of this feeling of loss, to move out of this feeling of meaninglessness, so that I could feel like life was a process of gaining and growing and that life was meaningful once again.

This was early on in my quantum leaping experiences with Corey and he surprised me with a technique, that although it would become all too familiar in the future, it freaked me out a bit the first time he did it. We were sitting, as per our usual, sipping tea in the sunlight on his deck in Colorado, looking out at the meadows, forests, rocky outcroppings and wide expansive sky and talking.

"So C, I know you're struggling. Hurting. I can see it in your eyes. I want you to remember this and to look for it. You are going to see it in the future, in men and women who need your help. When someone suffers a divorce, death, or loss like this, if they are okay, healthy, moving through it well, with alignment and acceptance, you will see a clarity in their eyes, even a potential sparkle. If they are struggling, hurting, resisting inside, you will also see this in their eyes, a shadow, like the left over redness and swelling from crying, but it may be only energetic. Still, you can see it. This is how you look C." Then he reached across the table, slapped me on the forehead and shouted, "Now!"

My eyes snapped shut automatically from the slap and when they opened a second later, I was watching my deceased brother Bart hand me an AA coin and I was listening to him tell me about the Serenity Prayer.

"If you can't change your reality, you have to accept it." Bart had said to me.

I looked down at the gold coin lying in the palm of my hand and read the embossed words:

God grant me the serenity to accept the things I cannot change.

The courage to change the things I can.

And the wisdom to know the difference.

"But really Corey, it takes more than acceptance. You've got to do more than that. You have to embrace what you can't change." I was hearing Bart again, the same words, the same conversation we had so many years ago. I was watching him and hearing him tell me, again "Everything in life, ex-specially the bad stuff, is a gift. Your job is to discover that gift and then to give back to the world."

As he spoke, I realized I needed to do more than accept the divorce and the new shape of my family. I needed to embrace it.

And with that thought we swooshed again and suddenly we were back on the deck chairs, sitting in the clear Rocky Mountain air.

"Wow that was a trip!" I laughed. "So I quantum leap to you in the future and then we both quantum leap to other times in my past?"

"Sure, if we want. I may take you to a number of different times and places and planes, if I deem it instructive. Now, I'm going to send you home with this one insight: all of your pain will disappear and you will find your joy, when you stop resisting and start embracing your present reality with gratitude. And I really mean that C. All of your pain will disappear the moment you shift from resistance to acceptance, from regret to gratitude. So, here are two techniques to practice until we meet again C…"

According to Corey's directions I revised the first line so that it said:

God grant me the gratitude to embrace the things I cannot change.

And I began reciting this new Gratitude Prayer hundreds of times every single day.

God grant me the gratitude to *embrace* the things I cannot change

The courage to change the things I can

And the wisdom to know the difference.

Then I heard this loud rumbling sound like thunder and a smooth pouring rain, and felt myself being sucked through a dark tunnel and out into the sunlight. There in front of me, I saw Bart and I, as young little boys, maybe 12 and 8. We were at a lake-shore looking for and collecting rocks.

"Look Bart." I heard my younger self sing out in an excited voice. "A wish rock! A real one!"

A wish rock was any small stone where there was a continuous band of color, or different kind of stone, that went all the way around the rock without breaking. If you had one complete circle you got one wish—two circles, two wishes. The idea was to make your wish and then keep the stone until the wish came true. Sometimes we would carry the rock around for days or keep it in our bedroom for weeks or months and other times we would lose the rock later that same day.

Then the scene seemed to pause and Corey was standing beside me talking, his hand resting on my shoulder. "Now, just like those wish rocks you collected as kids C. I want you to find and start using a gratitude stone, like Lee Bower describes in his work."

"The way a gratitude stone works, is much like a wish rock. You find one, a small one that fits in your pocket nicely, that you like to look at and that has a nice feel in your hand. And you carry it with you every day, and every time you touch it you have to say and think and feel a gratitude. You will touch the rock at least twice each day C, in the morning and at night, when you put it in and take it out of your pocket. But you will also touch it and say gratitudes, repeatedly throughout your day, thereby causing you to live constantly in an attitude of gratitude."

"Now for you C, I want you to find one that is smooth and that you can hold in between your thumb and your index finger. Curl your index finger under the stone and rub your thumb back and forth on the stone, as you think and feel about your gratitudes. This activates an acupressure point that causes relaxation and a good mood and it establishes a physical trigger, or emotional anchor, so that anytime you repeat the action your mood will improve."

I found my gratitude stone along the rocky bed of the Mad River near my home. The water that washes over these stones is the same water we bathe in and drink in my home. The salmon we eat swim here and so do we, so it's fitting that my gratitude stone would come from here as well. It is a black, flat, smooth piece of shale with a white band of marble running around it in a perfect wish rock band.

After a few weeks, I was enjoying the gratitude stone and prayer so much, and was beginning to feel such a powerful shift inside me that I created a new technique of using gratitude spots.

To make a gratitude spot, pick a place that you walk by repeatedly throughout your day. For example, on the Humboldt State University campus my office was in a building at the top of several long flights of stairs. From the top of the staircase, the view off the hill and over Humboldt Bay is beautiful, even enshrouded in fog or wrapped in rain. I generally would climb these stairs 4-8 times each day and every time I got to the top of that staircase, whether I was alone or with someone else, whether it was raining or sunny, I would stop, look out at the bay and think and feel a gratitude. Sometimes I would stop for 30 seconds, sometimes 3 minutes, but either way my day was filled with consistent moments of joy and gratitude. Similarly in my home, I have a window with a view that I'm particularly fond of and every time I walk by it, I think a gratitude in the same way.

In addition to the gratitude stone assignment, Corey required me to write at least 10 things I was grateful for every day, listing especially all the reasons I was grateful for my new situation. Sometimes I would list 10 or 20, other times I would fill several pages. Sometimes I would list things that were true about my new situation, things that really existed like my gratitude for my boys, my job at the university, my parents, where I lived, and so on. At other times I would list things I wanted to occur. I would begin each gratitude with the phrase "I am so happy and grateful now that…" and then fill in the rest with whatever I wanted, as if it had already occurred. This particular way of phrasing an affirmation comes from Bob Proctor. His work was recently brought to many through Rhonda Byrne's book and film, *The Secret*.

At first many of these gratitudes were in the form of negatives "I am so happy and grateful now that _____ isn't happening anymore."

But as time went on they increasingly became focused on the present and the future in positive ways. I became obsessive-compulsive about saying and writing gratitudes. I filled entire notebooks, hundreds of pages with them, and rubbed my gratitude stone until it was smooth and shiny. I completely overloaded my consciousness with positive thoughts, saturating my brain with positive neurotransmitters and brainwashing myself away from sadness and despair, toward hope and joy. And I came to be truly grateful for my new life, and I came to recognize it as a blessed experience that I had manifested myself for my own good.

"Now listen up and watch C. This practice you are doing of taking that which appears the worst in life and turning it around with gratitude into a blessing, a gift, is so powerful that you can find it in every major spiritual tradition in the world. In Christianity this ancient wisdom is taught through the Beatitudes, the set of teachings by Jesus that begin with "Blessed are…" such as "blessed are those who mourn: for they will be comforted." Beatitude comes from a Latin root meaning fortunate, happy, or blissful. And it is related to the Latin, Italian and French terms for attitude and aptitude."

"What you are learning right now from experience, the powerful transformation you are enjoying by employing the constant use of gratitudes or beatitudes is precisely what our language is literally telling us. The secret of how this works is embedded in the language itself."

"Beatitude. Be Attitude. Be Your Attitude."

"Be it—Evoke, Create, Feel, Have—the Attitude you Want to Have."

"Can you see it C?"

"Yes," I replied in wonder. "The secret is right there out in the open, hidden in plain sight."

"Now listen C. Feel this: You must evoke and feel the attitude of success in order to have the aptitude to succeed. You have to Be In the Attitude of Joy in order to begin feeling joy in your life again."

"You can't just Enjoy. You have to Be In Joy. You have to Be In Joy with Life—in order to Enjoy life."

"The language is telling us everything. The Secret is hidden in the Language. All organic, and complex systems, such as language systems or ecosystems, have embedded structures and patterns inside their chaos, like the Fibonacci series of numbers in nature, spiraling patterns that we can see and understand with careful study, and once understood they allow us to predict, adapt and create."

"Once we see this pattern, we know how to proceed."

"Your Attitude Determines Your Aptitude."

"Your Emotions Dictate Your Abilities."

"Your Consciousness Controls Your Choices."

"Your Perceptions Proscribe Your Possibilities."

With those words still echoing in my mind, the colors before me swirled and I felt myself sailing back to my new life, armed, infused and overwhelmed with an aptitude for gratitude. And in time and with practice, that aptitude turned into an attitude and I became truly grateful not just for my new life, but for the troubles and losses I had suffered as well. And in fact, I realized that I had finally found the gifts that Bart was talking about in my own life and my own losses.

One of Bart's favorite quotes comes from Richard Bach's fabulous book *Illusions,* which had such a formative impact on us both growing up. In the book the main character is flying around the U.S. selling rides in his bi-plane at county fairs and small towns. He meets another man doing the same, named Donald Shimoda, who is a true messiah, an enlightened bodhisattva still on earth. He teaches the main character, Richard, how to walk on water, levitate and manifest anything he wants, as well as how to perform a host of other miracles.

In the end when Donald dies, Richard reads in the *Messiah's Handbook* which his enlightened friend had given him and discovers the transformational power of perception. The book tells him:

"What the caterpillar calls the end of the world, the Master calls a butterfly."

That quote is on a plaque at Bart's memorial high in the Rocky Mountains, not far from the deck where Corey and I sit and have our conversations. It not only signifies how he lived his life, constantly coming back from the edge of death, re-emerging as something new and more beautiful than before—It also illustrates how he crossed over.

I didn't realize it when he passed, but years later, after I began quantum leaping, I would see that the end of my old world which was signaled by the loss of my brother, my best friend, and my wife, would also be the beginning of a new world for me. I could not have known it then, but in the years to come I would move to a new home, change career paths, meet the love of my life, and regain the family I thought I had lost.

And most importantly, the real gift in all that pain, was that it served as such a powerful catalyst for my growth, for my learning, my gaining emotional and energetic mastery, gaining the ability to do, be and have anything I want in life, as well as the ability to teach others how to make their lives immeasurably better in the same way...

All along Bart was right, what I saw as the end, what we all see as our "end," our tragedy, is really our beginning, our triumph, and the greatest gift for our growth that we will ever receive.

In time and with gratitudes, I would eventually crawl out of my chrysalis, unfold my wings and fly.

We all do.

And you will too, dear reader. Your time is coming too. Your time is Here Now.

When would now be a good time to be grateful for all you have gone through, ex-specially the bad stuff and to feel the gift you have become as a result of it and give that back to the world in powerfully purposeful and fulfilling ways?

And since you already know that one day you will look back on all of your troubles and laugh, why wait to feel better, when you are already curious about how good it would feel to laugh now, as you take your lessons and gifts and pay them forward into your bright and limitless future!

CHAPTER THREE

EXPAND DON'T CONTRACT

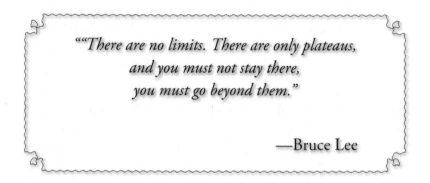

> ""*There are no limits. There are only plateaus,*
> *and you must not stay there,*
> *you must go beyond them.*"
>
> —Bruce Lee

During that time, I was practicing my gratitudes and saying my gratitude prayer each day, using my gratitude stones and spots and doing everything that Corey coached me on. And I was feeling better, but he wasn't done with me yet.

Once again as we sat talking and sipping tea, he transported me through time. "Look into your cup C, look down deep through the swirling shades of color to the leaves and dust at the bottom and let it swirl and move and change shape and form, until…"

As I looked down into the cup and my focus narrowed, suddenly shapes swirled and began to form. I began to hear a loud chorus of voices and I could see a football game playing on a big screen TV in a bar. Then I heard Corey's voice, shouting above the din:

"Now I will show you…How to Have Fun Watching the Super Bowl."

I had never really been one for team sports. I played some in school, but I was never a fan. I played soccer growing up as a kid and a few years of football in junior high and high school. But for me, I was always pulled toward individual sports: wrestling, gymnastics, and martial arts.

And I have always been one who is attracted to doing a sport much more than watching it. I mean, for me, I pretty much have always felt that watching a sport was like watching porn, a damn poor excuse for doing the real thing. I'd rather be in there on the playing field or in between the sheets than cheering or booing from the sidelines. So the super bowl never held any attraction to me. Most of my life I wasn't even aware of who was playing much less did I care who won or lost.

So there I was standing in a crowded sports bar, listening to the deafening roars, the cheering and cussing, the shouts of victory and the wails of defeat, as each team made a good or bad play. I found that I didn't really care to cheer when the "favorite" team did well, or to cuss or get angry when they didn't. It was all rather boring to me and I found it just as difficult to get happy about a good play as it was to get mad about a bad one.

I began to watch the people around me though. When a great play was won, they cheered, jumped up and down, shouted, spilled their drinks, patted each other on the back, and clearly were experiencing pleasure and joy and were awash in positive neuro-transmitters. When a play was lost, or a "bad" call was made however, they pounded the table, cussed, got angry, criticized the players, the coach, the world and anyone and everyone in it. Clearly they were experiencing pain and depression, and were drowning in a bath of negative neuro-inhibitors.

Now to be fair, there were some people who cheered at the victories and expressed a dislike for the defeats, but clearly were not moved out of emotional alignment by them. These folks might even complain on a "bad" play, but they weren't really angry. They continued to laugh and they forgot about the game and the outcome when it was over and just remembered the fun they had watching and talking with their friends.

"Now C, to have fun and enjoy the game you have to attach to it, to care about it a little bit. Even if you don't care who wins or loses you have to care enough to appreciate an athletic move, a great play or lucky catch. So in order to have fun, you have to attach a little. If you're bored, it's because you haven't found anything to attach to, to care about and be interested in. Now in this particular instance you might be a little too detached," he laughed, "and thus you're a bit bored."

"But for the most part C, the vast majority of the people here are so attached to the outcome of the game that their entire night (or entire week for some of them) will be affected by tonight's game. They are way too attached." Corey observed.

It was almost as if Corey's voice took over where my thoughts trailed off and then he continued to explain further. "As their 'favorite' team loses, and the game winds down, watch them C. They will veer right or left, into anger or depression, spinning deeper and deeper into negative feelings. And instead of going home and making love to their partners in new and inventive ways tonight, they will go home sullen and manufacture a fight and stay depressed and angry for days. Now does that sound like a good strategy to you?"

"Hell no," I replied.

"The difference between the happy people and the unhappy people, is those in the first group were detached from the outcome. They knew they were there to have fun watching the game. They didn't care who won or what happened. They were willing to celebrate the game no matter what."

"They understood as Neale Walsch tells us in *Communion with God* that failure does not exist. It is only an illusion. Bad plays do not exist. They are just a part of the illusion designed to make us happy. If our team made a touchdown on every play, it would cease to have meaning; it would stop being fun. The reason they fumble, get tackled and allow the other team to score is simply because it makes it more fun when they tackle, stop a touchdown or score one for themselves. The only reason failure exists is so that we can enjoy and experience success."

"Do you see my point C?" Corey asked, holding one finger up in front of my face and suddenly there was a swooshing sensation and all I could see was black.

I felt myself being tugged backwards and then I dropped down, back into my body in my meditation chair at home. As I opened my eyes and took a moment to adjust and get my bearings I heard my son in the other room, upset and yelling at his computer.

It was not an unusual occurrence for either of the boys to get so upset at their computers glitching out or freezing up that they would be pushed to anger or tears, exploding, screaming at the computer and slamming things around. In fact I've seen the same technology tantrums thrown by adults in professional offices and at universities. Sadly, I used to be one of the worst, but Corey and I programmed that right out of me as well.

After getting Hunter to take a break and settle down, I explained my new insight to him.

"So you see Hunter the game wouldn't be any fun if you won and got to the end all the time, super-fast without having to do anything. And you can always play the game again, another time, no matter what happens this time. You always get to re-spawn and start over. So when you die or something doesn't work right that's not a bad thing. It's actually a good thing. It's the only thing making the game challenging or in other words making it fun. So now when you make a good play or win or score, you can celebrate your victory and say 'Wow! Hurray, I totally did it! Awesome!' and when something goes wrong or you die, you can shout, 'Wow! Hurray, I died, what a great shot, that guy totally killed me, now I get to respawn and try again, awesome!' And either way you get to enjoy yourself and the game which is the whole reason you are playing it to begin with."

"The same is true of life. It really is just a game also," Corey had said to me. "The death on the video game is an illusion. It's not real. We get to re-spawn and play the game again and again, as many times as we want. This makes the game fun. It appears real so we can get engrossed in the action and pretend, or suspend our disbelief long enough to get into it and have fun and then when we die, we instantly see it was just an illusion, a game, and thus there is nothing to worry about."

"Yes, life is an illusion also," I replied.

"All of life is an illusion C, just as Richard Bach taught us through his character Donald Shimoda in *Illusions*. Life is like a movie or a play we have chosen to go watch or participate in. We suspend our disbelief for the time that we are here so we can enjoy and get engrossed in the experience. But one of the greatest reasons it is fun, is because we still know it's an illusion. We know that we are not killing during the heroic battle scene and we know that we are not dying in the tragic death scene."

"The secret then is to be fully engaged, playing with life, and still be able to see it as an illusion, a play, a movie we have chosen to participate in for a while. In the Buddhist tradition this illusion is called Maya and the illusory world of Maya loses all of its power over us as soon as we can see through the veil to the deeper reality behind the play. Then, even while participating in life and reveling in it, life can become a giant game of make believe, one that we can truly enjoy because we know we can embrace every experience that comes."

"You see," Corey continued, "when we chose to incarnate into physical form from the spirit realm, there were only two reasons for doing this. What possible reason could we have to leave a state of supreme bliss, ease and oneness for a state full of pain, disconnection and struggle? They are the same two reasons that you go to the movies or pick up a book or manifest any life experience: either to have fun (meaning to be entertained, to laugh, to feel heroic, etc.) or to learn something (to grow and learn and change in some way)."

"And in life you get to re-spawn just like in the video game. In Hunter and Bodie's video games we get more than one life. That's the truth about this life too. We get to manifest into physical form again and again, and we get to try out different choices on different planes of existence, so there truly is no such thing as death or failure at all."

"This is known as *The Universal Law of Opposites*, or *The Law of Contrast*. Here in physical form, we live in a world of contrasts, of opposites: Up and down, day and night, male and female, hot and cold, yin and yang, and so on. These opposites are always joined. They always exist together in harmony and rely on each other for mutual existence. One cannot exist without the other. So although we cannot have one without the other, we can learn to see and come to understand how they work together for the harmonious whole."

"Things become very simple then, once we bring this realization into our life. Every experience we face is either there for our pleasure or our learning. All we have to do is see it that way for it to be so and then we get to start enjoying whichever gifts it is going to provide."

"You see we enjoy our victories more than our defeats, but we learn from our losses more than our triumphs. Our greatest teachers, our most intense periods of growth, are generally found within our failures, our struggles and our most difficult of times. In fact, there is no such thing as failure only feedback, no such thing as loss only learning."

"I get it," I replied. "If I want to have fun in life, choose victories. If I want to learn and grow and become more than I am now, choose defeats. Either way, I win. I win every time."

"Exactly C. You Win some and you Learn some!"

Corey's lesson reminded of when I was an Olympic level athlete and national full contact martial arts champion. This is precisely how we viewed every competition. My best friend and training partner, Mark Selbee, who went on to win both the Heavy Weight and Super Heavy Weight World Kickboxing Belts, had a special ritual we performed after every competition. Before we could drive away and leave the parking lot after any fight, we would take the time to answer two questions:

1. What was working for me that I can emphasize and capitalize on in the next training cycle?

2. What wasn't working for me that I can fix and improve in the next training cycle?

In this way it didn't matter if we won or lost, we learned something from and enjoyed every competition. Using these strategies you will come to value your defeats just as much as your victories and you will easily and powerfully experience your losses as learning.

It is very important and helpful to be able to see the positive as positive and the negative as positive, to have this outlook of enjoying our successes and turning our failures into feedback for improvement. Not only because it helps you feel better as you look backward on life, but also and especially because it makes you more effective as you move forward in life.

When you are fixated on your failures, your mistakes, the things that have been done to you and that have gone wrong for you, it puts you into a scarcity mindset and a fear consciousness. When you operate from fear, your worst fears come true. When you operate from a vibration of confidence and success, you get those same results as well.

This lesson is first and most clearly taught in self-defense, in combat when you are facing the fear of pain and death from a physical confrontation.

Imagine: The big 6 foot 6 dude is standing in front of you cussing and threatening you and your loved ones and you are scared shitless because you are thinking "this is going to hurt," and "even if I win it will hurt," and "I may not win." And you are thinking "I may end up on the ground with him stomping on my head until my brains are washing the concrete, and my loved ones will be next..." This is the direction your thoughts are going as you look at him. And if you don't change your thoughts, it's the direction you will be going as well.

In self-defense and martial arts training we teach what is called "the warrior's mindset" where you replace those fear-filled thoughts with what you are going to do to him. "I'm not afraid of him, he should be afraid of me. I 'm gonna smash his throat and kick in his knee…"

You must in a moment like this replace prey thinking with predator thinking.

Whenever confronted with something dangerous, deadly, hurtful, something that is going to cause us some pain, like a fight or giving up an addiction or leaving a bad marriage or facing a career change, we will feel fear. Regardless of the threat, in order to respond to it you must replace fear with confidence. In order to succeed, you have to replace the fear of failure with its opposite.

Perhaps the budget cuts have come through, or the market has dropped and major losses have set in, or you have been fired. All of a sudden you are facing the looming giant of poverty, unpaid and unpayable bills, no money for electricity, gas for the car or food for the fridge and no job prospects. You don't know what to do. You see the cold street looming larger for your family and you, eating out of dumpsters, living under a bridge…..this is the direction your thoughts are going as you go about your day and struggle to get ahead. And this is exactly where you will be going, if you continue to focus on negative thoughts and fears, letting them spiral you down further and further.

As race car drivers will tell you, when you start spinning out, if you look at the wall you are going to steer right into it and hit the wall. Don't ever look at the wall. Keep your eyes on the open track. Look where you want to go and stay focused on what you want, not what you don't want.

So as Corey taught me, instead of spiraling downward, you must spiral upward. By any act of will possible, even if you don't believe it, you must turn those thoughts around and tell yourself, "No, we will make it through. This is an opportunity to get creative and motivated."

"Regardless of the specific details of the situation," he explained, "When you feel fear or pain you instinctively want to contract, to jerk your hand back from the hot stove, to curl up in a ball, in the fetal position and hide from this terror, from this pain. And a certain amount, a small amount of retraction or contraction may be necessary. You may need to dodge left or right or tactically retreat a step or two, or you may need to tighten the budget or move to a smaller house, but you must also expand. You must move into the situation with energy, confidence and forward, progressive, assertive, aggressive, attacking movements."

"Right Corey, the best defense is also offensive," I replied, remembering how GrandMaster Yi always taught us to use our blocks as attacks, so this philosophy was familiar to me.

"Yes C, the best defense pushes forward, stepping into the block offensively, attacking the attack. This is called what C?" Corey asked abruptly while staring at me intently.

"The Way of the Intercepting Fist," I replied automatically.

"Or it moves with the power of the attack, re-directing it and using its energy against it. This is called what?" Again he fixed me with an interrogating stare.

"Flowing Like Water, Sir," I replied smoothly.

He smiled and continued his lecture. "Often the best answer for a business losing money is to expand into a new product or service rather than to contract and get smaller."

"Often the best answer to the challenge of scarcity is the response of prosperity. Coyotes for example fill in what we call population holes. They have a reproductive strategy where the more pressure you put them under, the more you hunt and kill them, the more they expand, the more pups they have. They do not contract and have fewer pups trying to save just a few, but instead have many pups, extra pups, more than when times are good to maximize the potential for the greatest number to survive."

"When we are confronted with pain or trauma then, instead of contracting, instead of getting pushed into dysfunction, we can use it to push ourselves into hyper-functioning. We can turn the fires of destruction into the crucible that forges us into the hardest of steels."

"It's important to note that if we graphed most human learning or growth on a visual graph. It would not look like a smooth ramp going upward at a consistent angle:"

Growth or Learning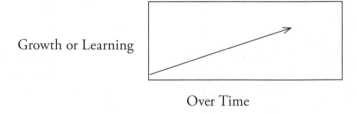

Over Time

"Instead we grow in fits and starts. We rapidly learn a new skill and then we plateau for a while before the next period of rapid growth or learning. So instead of a single line of learning or growth, we get a staircase.

Growth and Learning
and Resistance

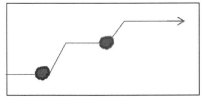

Over Time

"It's vitally important that you also understand that before each period of rapid and wonderful growth or expansion, there generally is a period of resistance or difficulty, a breakdown before the breakthrough. This is essentially another example of *The Universal Law of Opposites* and it could be expressed as *The Law of the Breakdown Before the Breakthrough*, or *The Law of Resistance and Persistence*. You will quite often experience the most resistance from the universe and other people, and encounter the greatest number of obstacles, right before your largest triumphs and the ultimate completion of your aims."

"Now that you understand this, you can get used to looking at each obstacle, each hardship, as an opening, an opportunity, a gift. In the Zen tradition (and now more recently in Parkour and free running) this truth is expressed in the koan "The obstacle is the path.""

"One way to effectively turn your obstacles into opportunities is to make use of or to enhance your natural ability for what has been termed Post Traumatic Growth. There are four kinds of strength or resilience that lead to Post Traumatic Growth: Physical, Mental, Emotional and Social Resilience. Even if you haven't experienced any trauma, these are the same four kinds of resilience needed to persist in the face of resistance and to push through the plateau to the success waiting ahead."

"First and most simply, the more you exercise, the more you move physically, the more you are improving your physical resilience. Movement is the body's meditation. Eat nutritious food, get enough sleep, drink lots of water and exercise every single day, and you will be more physically resilient than ever. You will burn off the stress hormone cortisol and release powerful doses of dopamine in your neurological system, which makes you feel more motivated and confident."

"Your mental resilience or will-power, your motivation gets stronger the more you exercise it, just like a muscle, so tackling a small challenge successfully, boosts your determination for larger challenges. Use small successes to motivate yourself and build up the momentum to tackle larger goals. Scientists have discovered that if you can experience three positive emotions for every one negative emotion, you dramatically improve your health and ability to accomplish goals and solve problems. This is called the 3 to 1 positive emotion ratio. So, focus on the positive to get through the negative and you will increase your mental or emotional resilience."

"Social resilience is the strength you gain from your social relationships with friends, family, neighbors and co-workers. Spending time with those people who make you feel good, instead of those that like to focus on your problems, allows you to have allies instead of enemies in your healing. In addition, touch and gratitudes are both simple ways to enhance social resilience. For example, shaking hands for six seconds increases the amount of oxytocin in your system, a hormone that enhances feelings of love and trust."

"So if we want to enhance our ability to grow from trauma, to expand when faced with adversity, we simply need to find daily exercises that will improve each one of these four abilities. Daily physical exercise and being physically active is clearly a basic requirement. Creating 'To-Do' lists and accomplishing one small task each day in the morning, or even accomplishing a task like a game, puzzle, soduko or counting backward from 100 by fives or making the bed, all will enhance our mental resilience. Using the regular practice of saying gratitudes or positive affirmations will strengthen emotional resilience. And making lists of friends, gratitudes about them, using touch and gratitudes more when you see them and so on, can all deepen and enhance those social relationships."

"Now that you are learning to see the losses as learning and your tragedies as holding the potential for triumph C, I want to connect this to what you already know."

"Do you remember all those thousands of hours training for Tae Kwon Do Nationals, the Junior Olympics, the World Cup? Do you remember all those mornings, thousands of them, getting up in the dark and going to the gym to lift? All those nights, running interval wind sprints and jogging down dark, deserted streets, or in the old University stadium?"

"Let's go there now. Close your eyes."

Immediately I could feel my heart racing, my breath coming in huge, ragged gasps, my lungs and muscles burning and suddenly I was there again, sometime during the 1990s, running through the dark, training. As I ran I could hear the stream of thoughts running through my head, my coaching voice shouting. I used to coach myself in my mind when training, shouting encouragement and yelling and screaming motivational phrases so that I could keep pushing, keep training harder and never give up.

"Push through pain. Fight through fatigue. Bend the body to the spirits will." I would say to myself in a constant refrain, when training and fighting, "When you're tired he's even more tired.

When you're hurt, he's hurting even more. Push until it hurts and then push some more."

And when running that same voice kept incessantly screaming, "Find the edge. Run until you want to quit. And then run some more. Keep on running with that quit inside you." The voice booming in my head as my legs burned like bee stings and my lungs ached and wheezed, "Because you're not training hard enough unless you want to quit. You're not pushing hard enough until you think you can't push anymore. You are not doing enough until you are doing the impossible."

On and on, around the track, or in the weight room, the same voice pounding in my head, screaming, "You can do this. You will do this. You are doing this. Now is the moment. This is the one. This is the workout, this is the one that will make the difference. You get up, you don't give up…" On and on and on, a constant, never stopping, endless litany of language, a propulsion system of impressive power.

"You remember C, how you used to push yourself through pain? How you used to talk to yourself so that nothing could stop you?"

"Yes Corey, I do now. I remember it all."

"Well C, this is no different. Emotional pain, physical pain, financial loss, personal loss, it's all the same. And to overcome it, we need the same techniques, the same intensity, the same unwavering focus and commitment. Do you remember Kerri Strug, and the 1996 Olympics?"

"Oh my god yes, that was one of my most favorite moments ever. She had just torn two ligaments in her ankle and couldn't even stand and had one vault left to win the gold and her coach, I remember, he was crazy: Bela Karolyi. He was standing there, his face just inches away from her face, yelling, screaming in this thick Hungarian accent, spit coming out of his mouth: 'You *can* do it! You *will* do it! You *can* do it! You *will* do it!'"

"And I remember watching her face change. It just hardened and became like steel, her eyes became intensely focused, on fire. And then she ran down the ramp on that ankle and stuck her double flip off the vault, nailing the landing perfectly and collapsed to her knees in pain, only to be carried off the mat, and later carried up to the gold metal platform by Karolyi himself. It was incredible!"

"That's right C, that's what I'm talking about. Without that broken ankle, without the pain that moment would not have been the greatest triumph of her life and one of the greatest moments in all of sports history nor would it have inspired you and millions of athletes around the world. Without the pain the pleasure is nothing. Without the tragedy the triumph is meaningless. So you have got to accept and push through this pain too."

"Yeah I get that, I understand Corey. I'll try."

"No C, don't try. Do. You know what Yoda said 'there is no try.'" Corey laughed. "Think about what Karolyi said to Strug. 'You *can* do it. You *will* do it.' He didn't tell her to try. He didn't leave any room for failure. Whether you are overcoming pain or fear or about to take on the impossible, you can never leave room for failure. You must believe to achieve."

Later that same year I told Corey about my growing desire to leave the University and he built even further on these teachings. It had become clear to me that it was time to move on, that I wanted something else. It was time for me to grow into who I was supposed to be, who I was destined to be, the author, speaker and personal development coach I was meant to be.

But, I had just received Tenure from the university the year before, which means they couldn't fire me. My job as a professor was secure. I finally had the elusive golden parachute that everyone aspires to and dreams of, especially those who have spent over twenty years getting a Ph.D. and a tenured position. It was a ridiculous idea from any perspective to leave the University, to leave the security of it, especially right after getting tenure while having two children, but I knew what I wanted to do.

I opened up our conversation with, "Well Corey, here is my plan: I've mapped out a strategy where in 3 years I could leave the University and replace my income with life-coaching and writing."

"Ok C, since you want to leave the university, how does it sound if we cut that time in half and double your income?"

"Wow, holy shit, yeah, I'd say that sounds great." I couldn't believe my ears. It was like somebody just told me my long-shot, lifetime dream, was a sure thing to be had right here and now.

"Ok C, let's do that then," he replied with a calm assurance as if we had just decided to go to the grocery store.

One year later, I was speaking with the Dean of my college and Department Chair about my resignation, just a few weeks before my last day. And they offered very kindly that I take a one year leave of absence to try coaching out, and if it didn't work out for me, then the University would have to hire me back and my job would be protected.

But I had already done my work and built my certainty. I had already created in myself the kind of faith that cannot be shaken that I would succeed. I didn't need any fall back options or safety nets. I wasn't moving forward into the challenges of the world filled with fear. I remembered Corey's lesson that I had to believe in order to achieve. So I reminded them about Hernando Cortez: when he landed on the Yucatan peninsula, his men were close to mutinying, so he had his ships scuttled, sunk in the harbor.

"Burn the ships!" He is rumored to have said. "Now, there is no way home, but through victory!"

When retreat is not an option, when surrender is impossible, when there is no way back, that's when we will dig the deepest and find our greatest strengths, and our most vital and powerful resources.

"Burn the ships," I told them with a smile. "I don't want any fall back options and I don't need a plan B. I will leave myself only one option: success." And so I left my tenured job at the university, with health and retirement benefits, with a guaranteed salary and students and institutional support, and left my twenty-years-to-earn-Ph.D. behind, because I was not worried about how I would succeed. I had given up fear about the How. Instead, I had created and grown into a new What and a new Why, so I knew the How would take care of itself.

When we have a goal that we must absolutely accomplish, when we are facing a challenge where failure is not an option, then we must have the fortitude to go all the way, to forget any thought of retreat. And in order to do that, in order to have that no-holds-barred attitude, no retreat, no surrender fortitude, we have to build certainty up inside us, build our certainty of success up until it is insurmountable, unstoppable, a force that cannot be denied.

How do we do this?

Corey built my certainty of success inside of me by quantum leaping me back to just one year earlier, to the day my dad died and I brought him back to life. After the familiar swoosh, we found ourselves on a bright beach in dazzling sunlight and I saw myself, standing in the surf and laughing.

We were on a family vacation in Mexico, with my Mom and Dad; Micki and I were still married and both boys were with us. We were body surfing and swimming when suddenly I heard my Mom scream out "Coreeeeeey!" The sound of her voice hit me hard, instantly filling me with fear and panic. I looked out to where my Dad had been swimming just a second before and there was nothing. He wasn't there. There was no sign of him anywhere.

I ran as fast as I could out into the waves and started searching for him. I was looking and feeling around in the water and I couldn't find him at all. For a second I thought maybe he was gone and that I would never find him. But then finally, I saw his hand, under the water, stiff and frozen like a claw. I grabbed it and pulled him up to the surface and as his face came up out of the water, I could see his mouth was locked open and his eyes were glazed over, covered with a film of death and I knew he was dead. Later the Doctors at the hospital would tell me that when the wave drove his face into the sand, it broke his neck and killed him instantly.

But just as surely as I knew he was dead, there was something else. It was like a voice inside me, like a voice in my head or some kind of inner knowing. And I heard it shout, with complete conviction and certainty, again and again: "No, this will not happen, not to mom, not again." Bart had passed only a year before this and I knew my mom couldn't take another loss. Hell, none of us could. I knew we needed my dad.

I remember as I was pulling him to shore that I was scared, almost freaking out. The shallower the water got, the heavier he got, and I was trying to support his head and neck and get him out of those damn waves as fast as I could. And when I finally pulled him up onto the sand, there was no pulse, no sign of breathing. There was nothing.

So Micki began rescue breathing while I did chest compressions. And as I knelt there pumping on his chest, every now and then I could feel this fear, a little panicked voice inside my head crying out "what if he dies, what if he doesn't come back?" But then, that fear would get shouted down by the other voice, the one that kept yelling "NO." It was absolutely roaring, inside my head "No, this will not happen. I won't let this happen."

It was wild. There was this intense knowing, this unshakable certainty inside me that kept shouting "No, I won't let this happen." It didn't matter to me that he had been dead for over five minutes or that I knew that CPR only works 8% of the time. I did hundreds of chest compressions on him and still there were no signs of life. But that didn't matter to me. I just knew, no matter what, we were going to bring him back.

Then, at what seemed like the last possible moment, his lips moved and he gasped for air and I saw that he was going to live. He started spitting sand out of his mouth and taking these little tiny breaths, and then, his eyes opened and locked onto mine, and I knew, my father had come back to us.

Even though he was already dead, I was certain of our success, certain we would bring him back. And bring him back we did. Today, he is still alive and with us, fully recovered and healthy, alive and vibrant, and every time I see him or hear his voice, I know that it is because of the strength of my certainty that he is here.

And years later, in precisely the same way, even though I had no evidence that I could replace or double my income, I was certain I would succeed. And succeed I did. Not only did I make more money my first year as a coach and professional speaker than I made my last year as a tenured professor, I also finished writing *The Art of Becoming*, edited and published a number of other books, found fulfillment and joy in serving others to get the lives of their dreams, had much more quality time to spend with my boys, and fell head over heels in love.

You can be just as certain of your success dear reader, if you can expand not contract when faced with fear, if you can build into yourself the propulsion system to take action, if you can see only feedback and never failure, then you will be able to overcome any obstacle in your path, then you too reader, like me, will have the power to manifest miracles and even to overcome death itself.

Now, when you put this book down I want you to remember a moment when you were certain, or a thing that you are certain of, something that you are absolutely certain about, something you know, or can do, or did, with unwavering confidence and certainty. Note how it looks, how close to you, the colors, how big the images are, and where they are. Note how it sounds and feel the feelings of certainty and confidence spinning inside your body. Memorize all of these and anchor them in.

Now think of the thing that you're afraid of or not sure about and put it in the same place as the first image. Make it look and sound and feel like the first image. Spin your feelings of certainty and confidence while you look at it, just like you did when you looked at the first image. Tell yourself "I can do it" "I will do it" "I am doing it."

And when you open your eyes my friend, you will be ready to run toward your life not away from it. You will be ready to expand into your obstacles and see them as opportunities as you remember that you never forgot the truth that "the obstacle is the path."

And you can feel yourself on that path, pushing through and over any and every obst-or-tunity, and as you do so, you will enjoy noticing how many other things that used to seem difficult or frightening start turning out to be easy and fun for you, until all you see before you are limitless, easy, enjoyable opportunities!

CHAPTER FOUR

THE MUSCLES OF THE MIND

*"There is nothing as powerful
as a changed mind.
You can change your hair, your clothing, your
address, your spouse, your residence, but
if you don't change your mind the same
experience will perpetuate itself over and over
again, because everything outwardly changed,
but nothing inwardly changed."*

—T.D. Jakes

I leaned back in my office chair and closed my eyes, taking long deep, relaxing breaths and began to countdown from 3 to 1, seeing each number in my mind and saying each three times. As I continued to deepen my relaxation I spoke to myself, "you are dropping down deeper and further still into your unconscious now can start learning and relaxing even further as you drop deep into your in Alpha level now that comfortable and familiar place where all things are possible."

Then, when I could feel that I had gone deep enough and reached Alpha level, I began to imagine myself floating up out of my body and into the sky to begin my leap. If you meditate enough, especially if you have someone to guide you into trance, you will come to learn what Alpha level brain waves feel like, at what level they vibrate and the quality of your awareness in this state, which is much like in lucid dreaming, and you will find it easy to recognize when you have reached the proper level. If you have never meditated at Alpha, or you are unsure of what it feels like, then I recommend you work with a licensed practitioner of Neuro-Linguistic Programming like myself for a few sessions in order to learn how to achieve Alpha on your own.

I flew through space, over the zenith of my arc and on down, faster and further, dropping toward the earth until I landed softly on Corey's porch.

"Sit down C, we've got a lot to talk about today." He opened.

"You bet Corey, I'm ready, lay it on me."

"Your mind is an absolute miracle, C."

"Understanding a little bit about how it works will give you the ability to take greater control of it, and this will allow you to begin making conscious and intentional use of even unconscious mental processes."

"First, it is helpful to understand how the mind thinks, or how it generates thoughts and emotions. Much of this is done habitually, unconsciously, without our awareness, so that many of our habitual patterns of thought and emotion are happening automatically, almost without our control. In fact, by the time we reach adulthood, most of our mental, emotional and behavioral reactions are pre-programmed into us and thus they are unconscious habits which we have little control over."

"Yeah, I get that," I replied. "Like cultural programming, the social morès and laws we follow; or gender programming, how we think we should act; or class conditioning, what we think is possible for us and so on."

"Exactly C. Now think about that for a moment: most of your thoughts aren't even yours. Imagine if most of your friends weren't yours by choice but were assigned to you. It's not surprising that most adults have some limiting beliefs and habitual ways of thinking and feeling that do not serve them or make them happy. And if most of our thoughts and feelings and thus most of our words and actions are made by habit rather than choice, then we truly don't have mastery over our lives."

"We are living by default rather than design, by accident instead of intention. We are living without freedom of choice at the most fundamental of levels."

"Now before we go on, I want you to think about this C. Studies have shown that you rise or fall to the income level of the five people you spend the most time around. And they've shown this happens with more than just your finances. You become like them—in almost every way—the handful of people you spend the most time around."

"This is called *The Universal Law of Equilibrium* which states that the universe likes balance and seeks equilibrium, a return to a homeostatic condition. If you increase the air pressure in one of two different chambers, it will naturally bleed off half that pressure into the other chamber until the pressure is equalized."

"With that in mind would you like your best friends and your lover to be chosen by society, the media, your parents, the government or others (who may or may not have your best interest in mind)? Or, would you like to choose them yourself consciously?"

"Would you like your most intimate acquaintances assigned to you or chosen by you?"

"Well of course, I want to choose them," I replied.

"Precisely, and who is more intimate than your friends? Who do you spend the most time with?"

"Me I guess," I offered.

"Yes, with your thoughts, my friend, with your own thoughts. You spend more time with your own thoughts than anything else on the planet."

"And *The Law of Equilibrium* applies here too. You become the thoughts you think most. You bring about what you think about. So don't you think C, it would be a good idea to consciously choose your thoughts instead of letting them be chosen for you?"

"Yes absolutely Corey, I'm all in. So how do these habitual ways of thinking and feeling form?" I asked him, "and, more importantly how do we change them?"

"Well C, just like the farthest reaches of the cosmos, your brain is filled with millions of electrically charged neurons. There are over 30 million in fact, that blink on and off like stars winking in the night sky. Each neuron is electrically excitable and when one is stimulated it connects with other neurons through synapses which could be thought of as little chemical bridges. A whole bunch of neurons can all be connected together with a web of these synaptic bridges and this is called a neural network."

"You can imagine these neural networks as pathways or roads that thoughts travel on."

"These neural pathways, or roads for thoughts, grow in much the same way that a path grows and expands with use over time. The more people who walk on it, the more obvious it gets and the sooner it will be turned into a dirt road and then a paved road; then it is straightened and leveled out and two lanes are put in, then four lanes are added and so on. Eventually instead of having a dirt pathway that is hard to see in the forest and hard to travel, we have a freeway that's easy to get on and almost impossible to miss."

"The same thing happens with our neural pathways. Specific thoughts travel along specific neural pathways. The more we think a particular thought, the more its neural pathway grows, making it easier to think that same thought again, and again, and again."

"For example, if someone is trying to quit smoking, every time they feel the urge to smoke and they say 'No,' they have strengthened, or paved, the 'No smoking' neural pathway, making it easier to say 'No' the next time. Every time they decide to smoke, they strengthen or pave the 'yes, I will smoke' neural pathway, making it easier to say 'Yes' the next time and harder to say 'No.'"

"So, the mind is exactly like a muscle. And if we want to strengthen specific muscles, what do we do?" Corey asked me.

"Well, in sports and martial arts, we usually find an exercise that works that muscle group and then we perform that exercise on a regular basis, repeatedly." I answered.

"Yes, that's true and check this out," Corey continued. "The exercise can isolate the muscle and strengthen it and be nothing like the actual move the muscle will have to perform in competition or real life. Suppose for example that I wanted to strengthen a specific movement like a punch. I could practice punching, with or without hitting anything, and the repeated practice would strengthen the muscles used to punch. I could also choose an exercise like doing curls and tricep extensions with free weights to strengthen those same muscles. What is interesting to note here is that neither the curl nor the tricep extension simulate in any way a punch; neither looks like a punch in any way. But, since they isolate and strengthen the muscles used in a punch, they are effective in strengthening the punch. Thus, even if the exercise is artificial, meaning it doesn't even resemble the movement we are trying to strengthen, it can still be effective."

"So, if we want to train a specific neural pathway, if we want to train our mind to naturally have particular thoughts or thought patterns, we simply have to find an exercise, even if it is artificial, that will isolate and exercise those pathways."

"For example, even if you don't believe it, even if it is an artificial exercise, repeatedly saying 'I am a nonsmoker' will begin to grow new neural networks based on that identity. Repeatedly saying, 'I enjoy breathing free and clear and easy. I enjoy being free from nasty smelling cigarettes and ashtrays. I always say no to smoking. I am so happy and grateful that I quit smoking successfully and breathe free now,' will help grow and strengthen the neural pathways that say no to smoking. Say this enough times and you will re-condition your mind so that the nonsmoking pathway gets bigger than the smoking pathway, and eventually it won't be artificial or pretend, it will be natural and for real, and you will believe it and act on it naturally and habitually."

"Thus, when it comes to strengthening the muscles of the mind, it truly is a case of fake it until you make it. When practicing to gain mental mastery over the mind we might pretend at first, but that's okay because, you have to make believe before you can make a belief."

"Once we are empowered by belief and we link this to repetitive practice, we can literally change reality. By going inside and changing the physical structures of our brains, we change our habits of thought, emotion and action, and thus we change our reactions to the world, and then our world begins to change."

"Remember, all change comes from within, C. Never from without."

"Okay. So how does it work then?" I asked. "How do you do it?"

"When we have an established pattern of thinking that we have habitually used for a long time that particular neural network gets stimulated or paved quite often, making it easy to habitually think that way. One way we can change this is to begin exercising or paving an alternative neural network. After we have exercised it enough, we will begin using it more often and eventually the old, habitual neural network will atrophy and fall into disuse, and we will habitually rely on or more automatically use the new neural network."

"On a physiological level this works because our neurological system cannot tell the difference between imagination, memory and reality. To the cells and chemicals in the brain that carry our thoughts and emotions, a remembered experience and an imagined experience, are the same as the real experience we are having in the moment. And even more importantly the neurons, themselves, cannot tell the difference between whether they have been stimulated by a life experience or a consciously produced thought."

"When the neurons communicate across the synapse they use chemicals called Neurotransmitters. These neurotransmitters are produced by your body and released by your brain when it is told to. If we have a pleasant experience and we laugh and smile, for example, the neurotransmitter serotonin will be released, causing us to be happy."

"If on the other hand, there is no real-world experience causing us happiness, but we still want to feel happy, we can stimulate that through an artificial exercise like smiling in the mirror and laughing for a few minutes. When we smile, the muscular movement itself releases serotonin, and when we see our smile in the mirror and react to it, and when we laugh and hear our laughter and laugh more, (even though we are artificially producing the laugh to begin with) serotonin is still released, and thus we become physically and chemically happier."

"Although we started out pretending to be happy, the artificial exercise actually creates real happiness that is indistinguishable from our response to a happy 'real life' event. In addition to making us happier in the moment, this simple exercise has also paved, or stimulated the growth of a neural network of happiness which will make it easier for us to access that happy feeling or state in the future."

"Let me give you an example, a real experience, because C, I want you to remember that words never teach, they can only explain. Experience teaches."

"Try this: Close your eyes and imagine walking into your own kitchen. See the cupboards, counters, and sink, and walk over to the refrigerator. Visualize opening the door and reaching inside to grab a glass bowl full of lemons. Take this bowl out and set it on the counter and take one lemon out of the bowl. Visualize lifting the lemon up to your nose, feel its waxy skin, smell its citrusy scent, feel the round shape filling the palm of your hand. Now take the lemon and cut it into a few wedges; watch the juice running out onto the cutting board. Smell the fresh sharp scent of the lemon juice. Now grab a juicy slice of lemon and lift it to your mouth and suck on it. Notice the taste, the tart and sour juice filling your mouth. And now feel your mouth exploding with saliva and puckering with the sharp, sour taste as more and more juice washes through your wet mouth which is now fully water-falling and..."

At this point, my mouth was watering, producing saliva, trying to manage the sour, citrusy taste it was experiencing. I encourage you, dear reader, if you're not already salivating to do that exercise now. Close your eyes and run yourself carefully through the same exercise so you too can experience how our imagination can create physiological responses, even to things that are not really there.

As Corey taught me, we can use mental images or visualizations in precisely the same way to consciously direct the body to release the neurotransmitters, hormones and chemicals we want. For example, since many people today struggle with depression or just aren't as happy as they want to be, wouldn't it be nice to know a way to help them, or us, to feel better?

There is a very simple and powerful practice that anyone can use to radically improve their mood, increase their overall level of happiness and combat depression. Several studies have been conducted where depressed patients smiled in a mirror every day for a fairly long period of time and within months experienced radical changes in their mood, increases in overall happiness and a lessening or complete loss of their previous depression.

One of the reasons this works, is that the part of the brain used to control the facial muscles that draw the cheeks upward into a smile is very closely related to the part of the brain that releases the neurochemicals that cause happiness, so even if the smile is faked and forced, if it is kept up long enough, it will cause a neurochemical change and thus an emotional one. In fact, the drugs we take to make us happy, whether they are prescribed by a doctor or bought on the street don't do anything but tell our brain which neurochemicals to release. And if we can accomplish the same thing with affirmations or smiling in a mirror and avoid the addictions, overdoses and side-effects that come with the drugs, then so much the better.

In fact there is an entire field of research called Laughter Therapy which is dedicated to studying and taking advantage of the beneficial effects of laughter on healing. Countless studies have been done and therapies applied that show how artificially induced laughter—whether through the use of film and theater, reading, laughter groups and so on—speeds the healing of the body, reduces pain in patients and creates a number of other beneficial results. In fact recent studies on biofeedback practices have shown that white blood cells, those that are most responsible for healing, are the most receptive to emotions.

The practice to cure depression, improve your mood and increase your overall level of happiness, then, is to spend 10 to 20 minutes, at least once, every day smiling at yourself in the mirror and laughing and evoking in yourself feelings of joy and happiness.

It is important as you feel those happy and joyful feelings to keep smiling and to really engage your facial muscles. "That means showing some teeth, my dear!" Corey once chided me as we engaged in this practice.

This combines the effect of both the physical response and the emotional response. So at the same time that your smiling facial muscles are telling your body to release serotonin and endorphins physically, the happy thoughts and images you are evoking are doing the same thing psychologically. I call this practice Physical Emotional Rehearsal, because it combines a rehearsed physical motion with a rehearsed emotion (or mental motion). Through such rehearsal we can train the brain and body to perform those same "motions" in the future, just as any rehearsal is practice for a performance. This practice, Physical Emotional Rehearsal is linked to Visual Motor Rehearsal which is discussed in other chapters of this book. If you currently feel depressed or unhappy, practice this technique for more than 40 days and the transformation in how you feel will be absolutely magical. In fact, you will feel it after just 4 days and even more intensely after 14 and if you want to really go for it, to get crazy happy with it, I dare you to do it for 40 days!

Do it and see what happens! Be happy and feel good for no reason at all!

Or don't. It's okay. There is no reason you would want to feel good for no reason, is there? Or, there is. You decide. Or not.

Once we understand the process by which thought and feeling patterns are formed, we can create new ones of any type.

If for example, you want to increase your confidence and your motivation, your perseverance to succeed in a specific, difficult or scary task, then you will want to increase the neurotransmitter dopamine in your brain and you will want to create a neural network that is based on thoughts and feelings of success, confidence and motivation.

The best part here is that you don't have to know the physiology that I'm explaining to you. You don't have to know that it is dopamine production that you need to increase. All you have to know is what feelings you want to have, what emotions you want to feel and what thoughts you want to think. Then by using an affirmation or a visualization or any number of other techniques, all you have to do is conjure up those feelings and thoughts. Those feelings and thoughts themselves, which you are artificially producing at first will stimulate the dopamine production and the growth of the neural network you want.

Or suppose for example, there is a couple that is having an argument and they are very angry with each other. At the moment, their brains are filled with cortisol, a stress hormone and it is physiologically difficult for them to think rationally and feel compassionately. If we want to help, instead of discussing the argument and trying to resolve it, we should first shift them out of anger and back into their feelings of love for each other. Then we can deal with the argument.

How might we do this? If we can stimulate the production of oxytocin, the love hormone, to replace the cortisol, it will naturally and automatically happen for both of them. One way to do this would be to simply ask them about when they fell in love, to tell us that story, and to tell us how they felt, what they loved most about their partner, why they were first attracted and why they got together. After a few minutes of talking about these memories the brain will be producing oxytocin because it is re-living these moments, re-experiencing them as they happened and falling in love all over again.

Whenever we use any of these exercises for changing habitual ways of thinking and feeling, or for changing an undesired emotion, we are conjuring up the targeted emotion we want so that we can saturate our neurons in the chemicals or neurotransmitters linked to that emotion. This neurochemical saturation is a physical process that literally changes the growth of our brain and yet, the process is started with the mind. Recent studies of what is called neuroplasticity have shown that even in adulthood the brain is constantly growing and changing and that many forms of meditation can affect this physical growth and direct specific changes in the physical structure of the brain itself.

Just as with any exercise, when we think of the mind as a muscle we recognize that to get stronger it takes repeated conditioning. We are all familiar with the Russian scientist Ivan Pavlov who performed a number of studies on classical conditioning. Most famously, by ringing a bell every time a dog was fed, he conditioned the dog to begin salivating anytime the bell was rung, even if no food was put out. This is a classical case where the bell becomes a trigger, or anchor, and evokes the physical response of salivating even though the original stimulus, the food, is no longer present.

Exercising the mind or training the brain for mental mastery is no different than training Pavlov's dog to salivate at the sound of a bell. With repeated applications we can program in a specific trigger, like the bell, to evoke a targeted emotion or state, or we can program out a trigger to avoid a habitually unhealthy pattern of thought. We also can train the brain to use alternative patterns of thought and feeling without the use of a trigger at all.

One of the simplest to use, but still one of the most powerful techniques for re-wiring the brain and creating new patterns of thought is the use of affirmations. Also called mantras or incantations, the use of affirmations dates back to before recorded history. Whenever we read in history about the use of spells or incantations to achieve magical ends or in religious texts about the use of mantras we are reading about the same thing: the repetitive use of language to change thought, feeling and behavior. The ancients of every culture on the planet knew about the magical transforming power of language and used it to their own benefit.

All of this Corey explained to me over tea and more importantly he answered the question on the forefront of my mind: How do you create a magical incantation, a transforming affirmation, to change your habitual thought and feeling patterns?

First decide on your goal, what you want to accomplish, or how you want to feel. Don't think about how you *don't* want to feel. Instead, frame it in such a way that you focus on how you would like to feel. So, for example, instead of "I don't want to be afraid of public speaking anymore," create a powerful mantra like "I am a masterful and charismatic public speaker who is calm and clear and audiences love me and I love the excitement and thrill of speaking in public and enjoying avalanches of abundant confidence and success."

Or, "I am a Champion. Each day I live the life of a champion. I eat, sleep and train like a champion. I am a champion."

During this same leap, Corey gave me one of my most powerful and favorite mantras. As we sat, sipping our tea and speaking in an unhurried and relaxed way, he slowly leaned forward, rested his forearms on the table and gave me an intense look, his eyes twinkling mischievously.

"You are, of course, familiar with the Zen tradition of Koan, I know C."

"Yeah, you know, the classics: What's the sound of one hand clapping? Or, are you and the mountain the same or different?"

"Who is dragging this corpse about?" He offered.

"What was my original face before I was born?" I countered.

"Good C. How about Seung Sahn Nim, *Dropping Ashes on the Buddha*, do you remember that one?"

"I remember two Corey: The classic and universal 'Just Like This' and then the very personal and often totally missed one 'How Are You?'"

"Perfect, everyone misses that one at the start of all his letters. And now one of my most favorite Koan of all time, a Grandmaster Yi original," he said as he stood and pushed his chair back. Then just as I was registering the blur of his foot flying toward my head, the old familiar words from GrandMaster Yi were flying out of his mouth: "You should have blocked."

Everything went black.

There is a tradition among the thousands of students and schools that GrandMaster Yi has given rise to of remembering and passing on his witty, direct and enlightened quotes. One of these sayings, one which we all repeat anytime someone gets hit is, of course, "you should have blocked."

I woke up in a dark movie theater to one of those, old count-down reels, the kind they used to run right before the show in the good old days, 5, 4, 3, 2, 1.

And then, it was like a movie montage. All of my Tae Kwon Do and Martial Arts training: it all spun before me, all the years, all the sweat, the blood, the books, all of it.

I saw myself at 11 years of age and at 16 and 24, kicking the heavy bag I hung in our barn and doing Gymnastics at the YMCA and wrestling with the team and going home night after night kneeling in front of a cinder block and punching until my knuckles bled and running and lifting and studying sports nutrition and researching everything from acupressure and biofeedback to ergogenic aids and the most effective sports-specific cross training methods.

I saw the years and years on the mat, learning and practicing and perfecting and teaching and inventing. I saw every competition, every win and defeat, every promotional belt testing and board and brick break. I saw the birth and rise of my school, the success of my students, the growth of the black belts and instructors under me and then the screen went black.

And all of a sudden, written in giant powerful letters all across the screen and thundering through the theater in his voice were the words:

Who is the Master?	I am!
Who am I?	The Master!
Who is the Master of my life?	I am!
Who am I?	The Master of my life!
Who is the Master of my Emotions?	I am!
Who am I?	The Master of my Emotions!
Who is the Master of my Career?	I am!
Who am I?	The Master of my Career!

It went on until I was shouting the mantra along with the movie and then I was shouting out the words and the movie followed me.

When the leap was over and we returned to Corey's porch, he was sitting in his chair laughing.

"Nice round kick." I said. "I didn't know you could smack someone in the head to induce hypnosis. But that mantra is powerful, I love it! It's perfect for me."

"Yes it is but, you don't have to be a Tae Kwon Do master for it to work C. Everyone, once they realize it, is master of their own destiny, their own manifested life experience, and this just reminds them of that. Its other strength is in its flexibility. It can be adapted to any situation or desire. So use it well and use it often."

"By the way, if you are lifting weights and want to get more out of your workouts, if you want to escalate, increase, improve, what do you do?"

"That's simple. You increase the amount of weight, the number of repetitions in each set and the number of sets in each workout and the number of workouts in a week." I replied.

"Right, you increase the intensity and the frequency. Do the same with incantations or anything." He said and then waved his hand and I was ejected up into the sky on my way back home.

He taught me that once you have created your powerful incantation it is important to repeat it several times every day, the more often, and the more times the better. Standing in front of the mirror and repeating your affirmation 5-20 times is one excellent method. Another or an additional technique, is to take a power stance or a specific pose, and make a specific and meaningful gesture with your hand (like holding your hands together in prayer or holding your hand on your heart), and repeat your mantra. You can also repeat it many times by writing it down.

Each technique works in slightly different ways so for the best results do all three. Looking in the mirror while saying and hearing the words helps us connect them to our sense of self, to our own identity through the visual and auditory senses. The power stance and the gesture act through our kinesthetic and auditory senses, helping us link what we are hearing and saying to our body, our physical self. And writing the affirmation down transmits the words and meanings to us visually and kinesthetically rather than verbally, so we take in their meaning and accept it in a third manner.

When you repeat your affirmation it is important to feel the feelings associated with it. For, as we learned earlier, creating those emotions ourselves will generate them physiologically in our body and link them to the affirmation and the newly forming neural network.

A slight variation of this is to write out a story as if your goal already has been accomplished, as if you already felt the way you want to feel. This is called pre-paving and you can think of it that way: you are preparing the roads in your new neural network for paving. Think about how you will feel, what you will think, say, do, and then write about it as if it has already happened. Fill in all the details you can and conjure up the feelings you will feel when you are successful.

It might help to think about this as a letter to a friend or a parent or yourself, a letter written from the future, starting out with your affirmation and then expanding to deliver all the details of your new life. Include in this write up all the reasons you knew you would be successful, all the experiences and abilities you have had that led to this future success, all the allies and supporters and resources that helped you get there. Just the act of writing this story or letter will stimulate the growth of thought and feeling patterns associated with it and reading it over every few days, or writing different versions of it, will reinforce them even further.

A final technique Corey taught me for rewiring the brain and changing reality is often called Powerful Positive Questions. Curiosity and questions, Corey taught me, vibrate at a very high frequency and forcefully attract answers. If directed and focused correctly, they can bring about almost miraculous results.

The way they work is this: you create and ask yourself a question, but do not answer it. Frame your question in a powerfully positive and optimistic way, such as "What is the most, or best, I could imagine....?" By framing the issue positively you are generating positive feelings and powerful neurochemistry around it and by framing it as a question you are opening yourself up to unlimited possibilities and allowing the universe to answer it for you.

Just after having learned about the power of positive questions I was at a large literary conference at a University and I was walking to a presentation with two other authors. We were each going to be sharing from our most recent books and fielding questions from audience members. However, at such large conferences there are many events going on at once and scheduled at the same time as us was a panel of world-famous authors, real fan favorites.

As we walked across the large campus toward our building one of my fellow authors said, "Man I sure hope at least a few people show up. I don't want to see an empty room."

Instead of indulging in that kind of negative thinking and talk, I briefly explained the concept of powerful positive questions to them and we began firing them off one after another as we walked:

"Instead of saying 'I don't want to see an empty room,' how about saying 'What's the most number of people we could imagine being there?'" I offered to start us off.

"Yes, what's the most packed we could imagine the room?" My friend added.

"What's the most number of chairs we can imagine having to bring in because there are so many people?" I asked.

"Oh yeah, and what's the most people we can imagine still standing in the back of the room because there are no more chairs?" The other author laughed.

"Oh, Oh, and what's the most number of people we could imagine sitting on the floor up front and standing in the doorway to the hall because there is no more space in the room?" I asked as we kept the litany of questions going.

We were laughing and joking and just having a ball with the questions as we set up for our presentation. Then as people began filing into the room, it became clear we needed to bring in more chairs. Audience members scrambled to help and we brought as many chairs as we could fit in the room. Then as more people kept filing in, standing in the back and sitting on the floor in the front, my friends and I stared at each other, eyes flashing in knowing disbelief at what our questions had just done.

In 10 years of attending that same conference none of us had ever seen anything like that happen. This is just one example of the power that positive questions have to call forth things into the world. They are truly magical.

I can recall at the end of that leap, Corey emphasizing the need for persistent training and the powerful results I should expect:

"After only 40 days with these practices C, you will discover that you have a habitual pattern of thinking and feeling grateful, confident and positive. You will find that you are tending to automatically react to things in a positive manner and that the constant chatter in your mind, that ceaseless internal dialogue, tends to be positive and appreciative and happy. This, as you now know and will soon experience after practicing these exercises, happens because you have intentionally trained your brain to grow new neural networks. You will have gained mastery over your mind."

"And once you master the inside then you can master the outside C."

"These exercises will help you gain mastery over your mind and over your thoughts and feelings. But remember, these techniques are just like any form of physical exercise; they only work if you work them. It is not enough to know how to do a push-up; if we want the benefits push-ups give us then we must do them, many of them, every day. So, make sure to exercise both your body and your mind every day."

And with that I rocketed back home, placed my fingers on the keyboard and began to write. I had a host of new techniques and skills and wanted to get them all down before I might forget. I was beginning to learn how to really train my brain, a level of mental martial arts that was yielding astounding results and I was eager to practice.

So remember, dear reader, it is key not only to monitor our habitual, chronic and persistent ways of thinking and feeling, but also that we work to master them so we can live by choice rather than by conditioning. Remember you become like the people you spend the most time around. And in precisely the same way you become the thoughts you think the most often. You bring about what you think about.

It is true that we are defined by our actions. And our actions are motivated by our feelings. And our feelings are created by our thoughts. So select your friends carefully and choose your thoughts with even greater care. Because your thoughts define who you are and determine your destiny.

I wonder, my friend, how eager you are to get started and how strongly you will find yourself drawn to practice these powerful techniques each and every day from this day forward, especially after you begin to enjoy the avalanches of abundant success and joy and pleasure they yield for you, as you practice them more and more and watch your life get better and better until it is beyond what you used to imagine and now know is possible for you?

CHAPTER FIVE

IT'S ALL ENERGY

> *"It followed from the special theory of
> relativity that mass and energy are both but
> different manifestations of the same thing —
> a somewhat unfamiliar conception for the
> average mind."*
>
> —Albert Einstein

"It's all energy C." Corey's voice echoed in my head as I walked across campus. Rays of bright sunlight bounced off leaves and made dappled shadows on the sidewalk at my feet. I often heard him talking in my head during those days as my repeated leaps and the growing months of conversations brought us closer and closer together.

"Everything around you is energy. That massive redwood, those gorgeous rhododendrons, even the concrete you are stepping on, it's all energy."

I had read a lot of Quantum Physics before Corey and I even began our conversations, so I already knew about how everything in the universe was made of energy. But I had never actually experienced it that way before. That is to say, until my conversations with Corey, I had never perceived or actually seen the world and everything in it as energy. But on that day, with his voice echoing in my head, I did.

At first I noticed a soft blurring of the shapes of the leaves as a light and almost completely clear aura became visible to my eyes. If you haven't seen auras before they are the electrical energy that all things emit and often the first auras you are able to see will appear translucent, a bit blurry, like a heat mirage on the road on a hot, sunny day. In time, you will learn to see colors.

As I looked more closely, I could begin to see the leaves vibrating. Not waving, like in the breeze, mind you, but each leaf, itself, the green cells inside it were vibrating. I continued to walk to work, allowing my vision to soften and my awareness to stretch out and I could see vibrating particles in everything that I looked at.

As I watched more intently, these particles became vibrating bundles of light and color, and soon the entire world around me had lost its solid form. Everything around me, from the ground at my feet to the trees and shrubs and the very air surrounding me was made up of tiny, vibrating bundles of light. I felt like I was in *The Matrix* seeing the code behind the illusions, the waves underneath the particles.

"This is the nature of reality C. This is the foundation of your physical world…" It was Corey again, in my head, lecturing me on energetics and warping my reality (both of which had clearly become favorite pastimes for him).

"In our last conversation C, I explained the physiology of how your MindBody Mastery techniques work—the way the brain and body change chemically and physically from these techniques. And while that level of transformation is powerful and important, it pales in comparison to the transformational speed and power at the energetic level."

"In addition to changing the chemistry and physical structures of the brain, the techniques we have been discussing also work on an electrical or energetic level, on the level of waves not particles, on the level of frequencies not things".

"Or more accurately, I should say, before the chemical and physical structures of our MindBody can change, they must change energetically first."

"The energetic level, you see, is foundational. Energy is the Alpha and the Omega, the cause and the effect. Energy is all that there is."

"Yes," I replied. "I remember studying this in graduate school. I loved learning that there is no such thing as matter in the universe. There is no such thing as things. There are no objects, no material reality, nothing to bump up against. Every 'thing' that we think of as matter, is actually a cluster of vibrating energy. Wild stuff, I love it!"

"Wild yes, but this is a known scientific fact, as indisputable as the law of gravity. At the subatomic level, there are no things or particles, only waves, frequencies or energies. This is important to emphasize and understand C. The science of Quantum Physics has been developed specifically to study what happens at this sub-atomic or Quantum level. Most of what Quantum Physicists have discovered and theorize about sounds amazing, miraculous and magical or just plain crazy to our common way of perceiving reality."

"Most of us see the world in much the same way as people saw it in the 19th century. We view the world as made up of physical matter, or objects, that occupy a particular place in space and time, and act on each other in direct cause and effect relationships. And while this view works most of the time, it not only is inaccurate, but it also misses most of what is going on."

"Every object or piece of matter is actually a bundle of energy. When we look underneath the atom, below the neutron, proton and electron, what we discover is that what appear to be very tiny particles or quanta are actually waves of energy. So every subatomic particle is actually a wave and every atom is made up of bundles of these waves."

"Energy is very real C. Energy is so real it is all there is."

"God is energy. And you are energy. And your spirit guides and your doppelganger are energy. And the magic mantras and the gratitudes and powerful positive questions are all energy."

"Love is energy and it is very real. Hate is energy and it is very real. Fear is energy and it is very real. Joy is energy and it is very real."

"And physical things manifest from energy events. Actually physical things are energy events."

"Are you beginning to see my point C?"

"Yes I am. If it's all energy then it's all about energy. Every problem, every solution, every issue, every technique: they're all about energy." I replied.

"Well said C. That's exactly right. It's actually another law of physics that physical things are manifested from energy. When enough energy coalesces in one place and time, it's what we perceive as matter or physical reality or what we might call a rock or a chair."

"Everything then or every 'thing' is energy. And every 'thing' or wave of energy is vibrating at a particular frequency." I offered, summarizing and repeating his points so they would stick in my memory.

This was something else that Corey taught me. If you want to truly listen to someone else, to truly hear what they are saying, and not just wait for your turn to speak, you need to repeat what they are saying in your own mind. Similarly, when you are introduced to someone and they say their name, repeat it back to them out loud and again in your own mind, if you want to remember it.

"Repetition, as Corey often said, "is the mother of retention. Repeat to remember."

"Exactly," he continued, "what we call matter is merely the material manifestation of the underlying frequency of the energy waves. In the same way that what we call 'your body' is really a collection of millions of cells and different species, what we experience as physical objects are really collections of ongoing energy events."

"So, you are energy. Your physical body is energy. Are you with me C?"

Periodically Corey would punctate these lectures with a quick question or a check-in just to make sure I wasn't fading. I had come to learn that these always preceded an important point, something he wanted to emphasize.

"Yes I got it Corey. Clear as crystal, I'm energy and my body is energy."

"Good C, so listen up, let's back up a bit and look at classical physics for a moment. First we have to recognize that even our most materialistic understanding of reality accepts the fact that there are forces, causal forces affecting physical reality that cannot be seen that have no material, physical existence. According to classical physics, not even Quantum Physics, there are only four forces in the Universe."

"The Strong and Weak Nuclear Forces in the Atom, Electromagnetic Radiation, and Gravity."

"Interestingly enough, these four forces cannot be seen. They are invisible. You can see their effects on physical reality, but you cannot see them, themselves."

"So if the strongest forces in our universe—in fact the only forces in existence—are invisible, doesn't it stand to reason that the forces operating inside us are the same. The strongest forces operating in us are not the kinetic movements of our body or the chemical processing of physical materials, but our invisible, energetic, thoughts and emotions."

"So each thought and feeling and memory you have is energy and each one is vibrating at a specific frequency and it is that frequency which determines the quality of your experience."

"And what we know from Quantum Physics is that if you change the frequency at which energy is vibrating, then you change it and thus you change the matter or the material manifestation of that energy."

"Sticking with classical physics for a moment, we are reminded by Newton's Third Law of Motion that 'For every action there is an equal and opposite reaction.' This is called *The Universal Law of the Karmic Boomerang*, or you get what you give, you reap what you sow. If you want to get more, give more. What you give is what you get. It is that simple and that powerful."

"Everything, all the things—including your thoughts—are energy. When you put out negative energy—or thought—you get back negative energy—or experience. And when you think positive thoughts, you get positive experiences. Energetically thoughts are actions."

"So thoughts *can* and *do* change things because they are things! Or really, not things, but events! Thoughts are actions all by themselves." Corey punctuated this last line by slamming his fist down on the table and rattling our tea cups.

"Before there was the hit, there was the thought of the hit. Before there was the automobile there was the thought. Before the I-phone and the internet, there was the thought that such things were possible. And that thought existed in only a few minds and now that reality exists in millions of minds and lives and trillions of dollars."

"Most often we don't believe this, or we miss this fact of reality. We generally tend to think of thoughts as being different from things and therefore we most often don't think that our thoughts can affect physical objects. But they do all the time, because thoughts and physical objects are made of the same 'thing': energy. Once we recognize that both physical objects and our thoughts are vibrating frequencies of energy it becomes clear that one can and does impact the other."

"On the Quantum level, thoughts, memories, feelings, and visualizations are the same as physical events and objects. Both are energy and both are equally real. This is one reason why the MindBody can't tell the difference between something we are experiencing, remembering or imagining. On the energetic level, all three are exactly the same."

"We have long known, for example, that the surfacing of a traumatic memory can have the same impact on a person as the lived event. It is not surprising then that a consciously created visualization can produce the same effect on the body, the nervous system and the brain as a lived event."

"Yeah Corey," I interjected, "whether it was my early biofeedback training or all the mental rehearsal we did in martial arts, both use this aspect of Visual Motor Rehearsal, but of course you know that, if I know it." I laughed.

You see VMR techniques have long been used in Olympic level competition and in martial arts, as well as in healing therapies. Especially in the realm of athletic performance these mechanisms have been well studied. It has been found, for example, that when an athlete visualizes herself performing in her sport, the same neurons throughout the entire body, not just in the brain, fire in exactly the same order as when she performs that same movement physically in practice or competition. Similarly, the same hormones and neuro-chemicals are released during the mental rehearsal as during the physical practice.

A well-publicized study of world class soviet athletes truly demonstrated the remarkable effectiveness of these techniques at the 1980 Winter Games in Lake Placid New York. After establishing their baseline average in free-throws, the athletes were divided into four groups, with each group given different ways to practice increasing their free-throw average: the first group spent 100% of their time physically training, the second spent 75% on physical practice and 25% on mental rehearsal, the third was split 50% and 50%, while the fourth group spent 75% of their time doing mental rehearsal and only 25% physically practicing. Remarkably the fourth group had the greatest improvement in performance, followed by groups, 3, 2, and 1 in that descending order, demonstrating that mental rehearsal was *more* effective in improving physical performance than physical practice.

As I explain to my Martial Arts students, when you are visualizing you aren't limited by gravity or your flexibility or by being tired or by a lack of strength, so you can see and feel yourself performing better than normal. You can experience yourself as having better balance, more strength and speed, and perfect technique. Then, since your body doesn't know the difference between your imagined mental rehearsal and physical reality, it begins to believe it can perform as well as you imagined it, and it remembers, in exactly the same way that physical practice creates muscle memory, our neurology remembers performing at this higher level.

I had used and taught these methods of Visual Motor Rehearsal for years before my conversations with Corey, but he was going to take me to the next level.

"Yes C, that's true. Now recall your Silva Method training and how the same processes of visual or mental rehearsal can be applied to non-athletic situations, experiences and feelings. The same is true of many techniques in Neuro-Linguistic Programming and the studies you have begun and will continue to do with Dr. Richard Bandler. We can use mental rehearsal to change or improve performance in any area of our lives, without limit. Period."

"Remember how in our earlier conversation I said that the brain could be changed by the influence of chemicals or neurotransmitters and also how each neuron was electrically excitable?"

"Yes I'm still with you." I replied curtly, so as not to interrupt.

"This is important because the body is not just a bio-chemical-physical system it is also an electro-chemical and electro-physical system. Although eastern medicine and philosophy has known this for thousands of years and calls this electrical or energetic component of the body chi or ki, western medicine has only recently begun to measure, explore and use this facet of the body in healing. EEG meters or Electroencephalographs for example can very accurately measure changes in thoughts and feelings by measuring the electrical currents produced by the brain."

"Scientists have recognized through the use of EEG meters that particular brain functions have specific frequencies. When we are deep in sleep or unconscious, for example, our brain wave frequency ranges between 0 and 4 hertz, or cycles per second. These are called Delta brain waves and they are the slowest cycling of brain waves and represent the deepest levels of sleep and mind. Beta brain waves, on the other hand, are much faster, cycling at 14 to 20 hertz or waves per second. This level of mind is associated with our waking consciousness and it is the brain wave frequency that we are in for most of our life. In between these two cycles is the Alpha level where the brain is cycling at 7 to 14 hertz. This is the level of mind you reach when you are lucid dreaming or just on the edge of waking and sleeping or when you have induced a trance state through meditation, hypnosis or other methods."

"Do you remember this from your Silva Method training and Neuro-Hypnotic Repatterning work with Dr. Bandler C?"

"Yes," I replied, I knew it well. "At the Alpha level you still maintain conscious control of your mind, but your brain waves are sufficiently slow enough to access the depths of your unconscious mind. In fact, at the Alpha level you are operating on both levels of mind and using both hemispheres of the brain which allows us to, as the pioneering work of Jose Silva and Dr. Bandler has shown, powerfully, quickly and permanently re-program the mind."

For readers not familiar with The Silva Method, it was first created by Jose Silva in the 1960s and is probably the most well-known meditation method on the planet. It has been used extensively by the US Military, and is currently practiced by over 60 million people in over 110 countries. Silva Method seminars, training guides, books and cd's are widely available and wonderfully effective in training you how to master your mind.

Although I had been studying his books for several years, my first personal introduction to the Silva Method came just two months after my wife left me. I knew that I was deeply heartbroken. I felt crushed, empty inside, visibly torn apart. I felt physically weak and vulnerable and had no spark for life. I knew I didn't want that feeling to last though.

I had seen friends spiral downward for years after their divorces before they began to claw their way back up again and live and grow and become happy and healthy. I resolved immediately not to lose several years or even a few weeks of my life to depression and victim-hood. I also recognized that I might need a little help in order to do that, so I enrolled in a Silva Method seminar, drove the five hours to San Francisco and returned home after two days a completely changed man.

As I drove back across the Golden Gate Bridge, thin clouds of fog blew through the burnt red cables and towers of the bridge and I turned north, headed for home. I knew as I drove that I was carrying with me one of the most powerful methods for mastering the mind that I had ever learned, a method I still use to this day. The Silva Method is, in fact, the foundation upon which Burt Goldman built his technique of quantum jumping and informs the method I used to quantum leap to talk with Corey.

Corey interrupted my reverie and continued. "The key difference between working at the Alpha level to re-wire the brain and most forms of therapy is that they only work on the Beta level of the mind, on the conscious mind and the left hemisphere. When we work at the Alpha level however, we are able to speak directly to the unconscious mind, using both hemispheres of the brain equally and thus we are able to re-program the mind faster and more permanently because we are working on an energetic level."

"So if you truly want to affect physical material reality, you could work with the 'stuff,' the material objects of life or you could go straight to the source. You could work with energy."

"And that's precisely what these methods are all about, working with energy, working with energy first, and foremost, and then with physical reality when it manifests. This is a much more efficient method of going about things, I've found, because energy is so much more responsive than dull matter. It works so much more powerfully and quickly."

"A simple illustration might serve here to explain how the physical structures of our brain, how our thought patterns are changed on an energetic level. Let's pretend for example that you have a fear of heights and every time you look off any high place, you are filled with gut wrenching fear: you get dizzy, and begin feeling nauseous and have the cold sweats."

"Two classical approaches for getting rid of this phobia might be to use psychoanalysis or behavioral conditioning. In psychoanalysis we would discuss and explore the phobia until we uncovered its origin in some earlier trauma and we would hope that this new understanding would somehow make the fear go away. In behavioral conditioning, we might expose you in various ways to increasing heights while reassuring you of your safety and hope that bit by bit the fear goes away. Both methods have been used historically to varying degrees of success and both tend to take a long time and repeated treatments in order to work, if they every work at all."

"On an energetic level, at the Alpha level however, we can work much faster. We don't need to talk for months to uncover the hidden trauma in the past. In fact, we don't even need to know the origin of the fear. All we have to know is what the fear feels like or what its vibrational frequency is. Similarly, on an energetic level, we don't need repeated treatments over a long period of time to change the fear. All we have to do is change the vibrational frequency once and it will remain changed forever."

"You see the fear, the phobia, has a very specific energetic or vibrational frequency. The feelings and thoughts associated with it are all vibrating at this same frequency. If we tap into this frequency by recalling our fear, then we can then change it."

"How do you think we change it C?"

"We go to Alpha level, of course." I replied.

"Yes, first we get ourselves to Alpha level then we can recall a memory of being afraid and turn down the power of the fear-filled frequency. Then by recalling a memory of being safe, confident and excited, we can call up a different frequency and replace the fear filled frequency with the safe one. When we replace the fear filled image or thought with the safe one, the vibrational frequency of the first thought will change and it will align with the second."

"There are a variety of ways this can be done, but once the vibrational frequency of the thought pattern has been changed, it will remain changed forever. And just like changing the dial on your radio to a new station, the only thoughts and feelings that will be broadcast are those linked to the new frequency."

"This new vibrational frequency, then, will stimulate the body, just as I described earlier, to release the chemicals linked to the safe thought and to grow the associated neural network and the phobia will be permanently gone."

"Soon C, you will be studying under Dr. Richard Bandler again, the creative genius behind the field of Neuro-Linguistic Programming and you will learn his Fast Phobia Cure."

Dr. Bandler made a name for himself early in his career by putting out ads for anyone who had a documented phobia that had been incurable for over 10 years. Psychiatrists brought him their most serious patients, others he visited in mental hospitals or their homes, and with each and every one, they walked away from a single meeting with Richard and their phobia was completely and permanently gone. Today the International Society for Neuro-Linguistic Programming, of which I am a member and trainer, conducts trainings in dozens of countries and has hundreds of thousands of members.

From time to time, Corey would tell me about things he had done or learned in his past that were still a part of my future. Now, even after years of working with Dr. Bandler I can still remember the first time I met him. He both looked and energetically felt scarier than hell, like a powerful wizard who could crush you with a single look or spell. At the same time though it was clear how much love and joy emanated out of the man. The sheer genius in how he worked with people and got them to change so gracefully and so quickly was remarkable. And the number of people who I watched transform after working with him was incredible.

That day Corey taught me one version of Dr. Bandler's Swish Pattern by doing it on me.

After having me drop into Alpha with a few deep breaths and the use of his own hypnotic voice and Neuro-Linguistic Programming language patterns, Corey told me to "Close your eyes and go back to one of those times when you were feeling bad, in the marriage or about the divorce, see it now on a movie screen in front of you and play that movie forward to the end, see what you saw and hear what you heard and said."

"Now, run the movie backward and play some silly carnival music over the top and see how ridiculous it is. Now reach up and grab that contrast knob, the one that turns the screen all black and white and when I count to three, flip the screen all white, then black, a bunch of times, back and forth, ready, one, two three, flip, flip, flip, flippety-flippety-flip, that's right. Now call up that image and the feelings associated with it and on the count of three you are going to throw it to the end of the universe, you are going to watch as it flies so far away from you it shrinks and shrinks until it disappears, ready, one, two, three, swish, oh its going, it's going, it's gone.

"Now, I want you to call up an image of you being happy and grateful and healthy after the divorce, of you still having loving relationships with your boys and a new romance for yourself, and spin those good feelings of pleasure bigger and bigger, now anchor that feeling in, right into that image, and anchor that good feeling into that image so you've got it."

"Now shrink that image down to the size of a postage stamp and put it in the corner of that other bad memory from before. Now on the count of three, the small good image is going to explode in size and shatter the old, bad feeling image and then the good image is going to get bigger and brighter and closer as the feelings get better and stronger and stronger, ready, one, two, three, swish!"

"Now pull that good image closer and make it bigger and brighter and anchor those good, spinning feelings in as you realize that you have already shifted and from this moment forward you are clear and full of gratitude and joy for everything you had and shared in your marriage and for the wonderful changes you have gone through and are going through, as you begin to wonder how much better things can get and how much better you can feel, as you find that the only question you have left to ask is How much pleasure can I stand?"

While Corey spoke, I could feel the images moving in front of me, the energy of emotions spinning inside of me and as we moved through each exercise I could feel physical shifts occurring inside of me. I could feel my vibration changing, the frequency at which I was waving quickened and gained a more harmonious rhythm, as my emotions spun the opposite direction, oscillating at a completely different frequency and suddenly I felt completely different."

I was thinking new thoughts about what my divorce meant, feeling new feelings, and in the place of anger, and hurt and blame, I was vibrating with joy, gratitude, understanding and love.

The channel had literally been changed. The frequency of the wave's vibration changed and everything I was thinking and feeling changed just as radically as changing the channel on the TV.

Over time, after I started training with Dr. Bandler personally, I came to recognize that much of what Corey was doing to me he had learned from Richard (or I was learning from Richard). I remember saying after my very first NLP seminar with Dr. Bandler that "NLP was the Silva Method on Steroids." Hands down, it is the most exciting and powerful of mental technologies I have ever encountered. A few of my favorites of Dr. Bandler's books include *Richard Bandler's Guide to Trance Formation, Time for a Change,* and *The Secrets of Being Happy.*

"Now remember C, once you change the energy you're giving out, you will change the energy and material manifestation you are getting back. When you change the energetic frequency of your thoughts, your feelings and actions change and thus the results you get boomeranged back to you from the world change."

"As you know from martial arts, when you push someone, they will push you back; when you pull on them, they will pull on you. The same is true in all of life."

"And the easiest level to work on is the most fundamental, the most malleable: the energetic level." Corey reminded me.

"So if you want to change anything in the physical world change your energy around it first."

One of the most powerful and wonderful parts of this process is how easy it is to work with energy. Since your thoughts and feelings are energy, all you have to do to work energetically is to call up different thoughts and different feelings.

Think of each thought as an electrical signal. And think of each feeling as the power behind that signal.

If you want to excite the neurons in your brain, for example that are linked to joy and happiness, you simply have to think and feel joyful thoughts and feelings. One of the easiest ways to do this is to recall or imagine a joyful scene and to call up those emotions in yourself. As you call up these thoughts and emotions, you are sending electrical signals to the neurons linked to happiness and joy and you are exciting them into action. As they fire more often and more serotonin is released, you will feel better in the moment and you will be growing a stronger neural network linked to happiness, making it much easier to think and feel happy in the future.

As Corey taught me, the powerful energetic force of our thoughts can and does, do much more than just control our feelings, behavior and physiology. The energy of our thoughts is always affecting material reality in direct and powerful ways. Since everything that has physical form in your life—every event, person, and object—is really a wave of energy vibrating at a specific frequency, its frequency can be affected by your thoughts.

One of my favorite uses of this from the Silva Method is called Programing Water.

You see water is easily influenced by energy including our thoughts. In his bestselling book, *The Hidden Messages in Water,* Dr. Masaru Emoto demonstrates this powerfully with his research on and photographs of freezing ice crystals.

Dr. Emoto began by photographing the crystalline structure of ice crystals with a microscope and comparing them to water taken from a variety of locations and saw astounding results. Water from natural springs and streams always produced fully complete and geometrically patterned and beautiful crystals, whereas the water from polluted places or tap water from Tokyo never formed complete crystals and had very incomplete, non-geometrical and ugly patterns.

Then they began experimenting with the same water, taking distilled water and saying different things to it and then photographing the crystals that formed. They found that in every language they tried, positive words of kindness, love and compassion always formed complete, beautiful and geometric crystals, whereas negative words of criticism, shame or hate always produced incomplete and ugly patterns. Words like "Thank you," "I love you," "I am sorry," all produced beautiful patterns, while words like "You fool," "I hate you," or water exposed to television or computers all produced incomplete and ugly patterns.

As Dr. Emoto explains it, all things have their specific vibrational frequencies, including words. And because water is so sensitive, it is strongly affected by these frequencies and records them. In fact, Dr. Emoto concludes that "water has the ability to copy and memorize information."

One extremely beneficial way we can make use of this energetic and informational recording power of water is when we have a question we want an answer to or a problem we are not sure how to solve. Before going to bed at night, get a class of clean water and put it next to your bed. Lie down and relax yourself down into Alpha level. Then sit up and hold the glass of water in both hands and focus on it, as you repeat your question over and over again. The water will record the energetic frequency, the specific vibration of your question. Drink half of the glass and then lie down and go to sleep. When you awake in the morning drink the other half of the glass.

Then as you go about your day, be open to the ideas coming to you because the solution to your problem will have been recorded in the water and it will now be inside you, waiting for you to become aware of it. Because like frequencies attract each other and because of water's ability to record information, the question you program into it will resonate with and attract its own vibrational match, its own answer. And in the morning that answer will be there waiting for you.

It's also very important to note that the human body is made up of over 70% water. We are primarily water. So, the words we say to ourselves, our thoughts and feelings are all energetic frequencies that are constantly programming the water inside us. In fact, they are influencing the entire universe around us.

A positive word or thought has the power to heal, improve and connect. A negative word or thought has the power to hurt, disconnect, and destroy.

The conversations we were having together on Corey's deck were connecting countless dots for me. Experiences I had in the past, things I had read or studied at one time, they were all starting to connect, to make sense to me.

As he spoke, I watched the bright sunlight beam back up from mica and quartz in the granite rock of the mountains and twinkle and burn on the edges of bright green leaves and pine needles. Even the air in front of my eyes seemed to be sparkling as tiny dots of golden light danced before me. Everything seemed to be glowing, vibrating, pulsating, waving in and out of form, flowing through existence.

"Are you with me? Do you got it C? This is just the beginning of learning how your thoughts energetically influence the world and the entire universe surrounding you. You are like a magician who can conjure up a spell with your mind and use it to change the physical world before you. You are like some wizard playing with electricity and unseen energies when you play with your thoughts in this manner. We all are."

As he spoke I could see waves of energy radiating out from me, interconnecting with all the other vibrating waves of energy surrounding me. I had already experienced some truly miraculous and magical changes in my life as a result of Corey's energy work, but this was as if an entirely new door into a different reality had been opened. I waved my magic fingers before me and laughed as I thought back to third grade when I wanted to be a sorcerer. Apparently I was on to something, even then.

What latent and until now invisible energies and untapped resources are you holding inside you, dear reader?

Can you feel the vibrating frequency of what you want in life and who you want to become?

Can you feel its pulsing rhythm, its unique pace, rising now up your spine, tingling, electrifying and charging you up like a lightning bolt of uncontrollable, unstoppable energy?

Tonight when you sleep, my friend, there will be a spinning, vibrating wheel of thought and energy in your mind, in your unconscious. A machine—a thought and idea generator—is being built and installed there, so that from now on it will constantly be turning, spinning out new, inspired ideas so that you easily and consistently receive consciously your own brilliant solutions which will and already are bringing you happiness without measure.

CHAPTER SIX

YOU ARE LIVING OUT A STORY

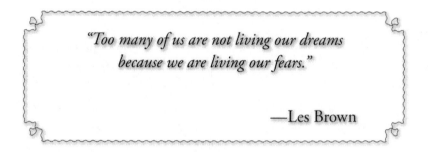

*"Too many of us are not living our dreams
because we are living our fears."*

—Les Brown

For this conversation Corey and I were down by the pond, skipping stones across the water, instead of sitting up on his deck as usual. We took turns, finding flat stones and zinging them side-armed out across the surface of the water.

"You know Corey," I said, "This reminds me of that video that was going around on the internet, called 'Liquid Mountaineering.' It was the one that looked like a short documentary on these guys from Portugal who had invented a new sport: running on water. It was so cool looking, you could see them running out and across the water for like thirty feet. And in fact it was all a hoax, a clever commercial for Hi-Tec shoes."

"Yeah, I remember that C. It was cool. It looked so real, it really made you believe, didn't it?"

"It did make me a believer Corey, yeah. Even with everything we know today about special effects and camera tricks, they still made it seem possible, made it look real."

"That's true C. Even though we have been taught to be very cynical and skeptical by modern culture that is not our true nature. You see our true nature is not to doubt. It is to believe. To make believe. And that is our greatest power not our greatest weakness as some skeptics and rationalists would have you believe."

"Human beings have something that no other animal has, something that no machine or computer will ever have: we have the power of imagination. And this is no small thing. Imagination gives us the power of Gods. Imagination allows us to see into the future. Imagination allows us to see that which does not exist and it opens up the possibility for us to call whatever we imagine into existence. Anything you can imagine you can create."

"All of our mystical traditions and major religions have recognized this. It is written in the holy scriptures of countless cultures that God is a Creator. That we were made in the Creator's image. And that we have some aspect of the Creator's unique power."

"Imagination—the ability to create that which does not presently exist—Imagination—the ability to make something out of nothing—is that power. And you have that power."

"Do you remember when you were a kid in Ft. Collins C? How all the neighborhood kids would get together and have those epic, mock battles?"

"Yes, I remember it all Corey. Bart and I, and our best friends Rick and Ken, and all the other kids in the neighborhood would get together down by the lake and play. There must have been a dozen of us at least. We would make up these complicated storylines of fantasy and adventure and have massive battles that would last for days. We might have to break for dinner to go home to our separate houses, but the next day, we would all meet back up and start the battle again from where we left off. It was awesome!"

"And during those battles there were many glorious victories and defeats, daring rescues and heroic deaths, weren't there C?"

"Oh yeah definitely. We would follow those narratives faithfully, playing each storyline out to the end, to either total victory or a glorious and prolonged death with swords sticking out of you as you tragically and bravely urged your comrades on! 'Go on without me' we would say heroically as we lay dying with arrows and spears sticking out of our bodies. Yeah, it was ridiculously fun, epic! We were definitely legends in our own minds," I laughed.

"Well you know C, things never really changed. In fact, they are the same for everyone. We are all legends in our own minds. We are all living out a made up story."

"Every single one of us, whether we are aware of it or not, is living out our own story."

"We have collective stories about ourselves as members of particular groups, nations and peoples. And more importantly, we have individual stories about ourselves personally. We each have a story for our lives, a story for who we are, where we are and how we got here."

"Sometimes these stories change or they have different chapters. And sometimes we are aware of the story we are living in, but most often, most people aren't."

"For example, for one time in our life, the story of our life was that Corey was a scholar-warrior, a martial artist dedicated to becoming a champion and a master and a scholar. It was, as you will recall, our entire being, our complete identity, our total focus. It affected every aspect of our life from what we ate, to how often we worked out, what books we read and philosophies we studied, where we went to graduate school and so on. And it was just a story that we chose. And it was a good one. And we enjoyed it immensely. And it was completely arbitrary. And it was one of an infinite number of stories we could have chosen."

"Many people, however, aren't aware that they are living out a particular story much less that they have complete freedom and power to choose whatever story they want to live."

"The secret is you can live any story you want to. You can consciously choose what life story you will live and what role you will play in it, villain, victim or hero. There are no limits to the possibilities."

"In fact, the saddest truth is that most people are living out a story that they don't like and they aren't even aware that they are the ones writing it, creating it. And anytime they are given a chance, they will tell anyone who will listen all about it."

"You know the kind of story I'm talking about: 'The world is so unfair, I got fired from my job. I have health problems. He treated me wrong,' on and on and on, they will go with their tragic story, repeating it, retelling it, complaining about it and living it. And they'll tell it to anyone who will listen: their hairdresser, the clerk at the grocery store, to you when they sit next to you on a plane or bus and so on. Man, it's ridiculous!"

"What I want you to realize, is that lately you have been telling yourself a stupid and tragic story and you would be a lot happier if you told yourself a different one. Now, you tell me C, what's your stupid story?"

"I know what you're talking about Corey. You mean the one about me being a victim, being broken-hearted from divorce, being lonely and missing my dead brother and best friend."

"Yup C," he laughed. "That's the dumb one. You and I both know that's a stupid, boring, disempowering, make-you-feel-like-shit story. And you call yourself a writer? Really, you can do a lot better than that."

"But it's true Corey," I protested.

"True? Ha!" he scoffed. "The truth changes. The truth is determined by your perspective. It is the meaning you assign to the facts. The facts never change, but the Truth, now that changes all the time. Take General Custer, for example: The facts are he killed thousands of Native Americans. The Truth at that time was that he was a defender of settlers and civilization. The Truth now is that he was a genocidal maniac."

"And I know that you are going to point to all these examples, all this 'evidence' that your story is 'true.'" Corey said in a whiney and wimpy voice. "But what you need to realize is that the popular phrase 'seeing is believing' has it all backward. The truth is 'believing is seeing.' You see whatever the story tells you to see."

"If you destroy that story and create a different one, you will see things differently, and more importantly you will feel differently and then you will behave differently, and then you will be living a different and better story. You will be living the life you want."

"You see, many people are walking around telling themselves similarly tragic and self-defeating stories. Stories like 'I'm too short, or too fat, or I'm too stupid, or I can't help it that I'm depressed or angry or an addict because of this thing that happened in my past.' But all of it can be changed."

"Every aspect of your story can be changed including even the physical form of your body. You should know this C. You know how radically you changed your body through years of dedicated weight lifting. And even if you never work out again, your body is and will remain permanently changed."

"But most people never succeed in changing the story that they hate living for three simple reasons:"

"First, because they don't know that they can."

"Second, because they are too attached to the familiarity of the old story and afraid of change and that which is new."

"And third, because there is a secondary benefit they are getting from their story: the victim gets to believe he or she is right and innocent, the depressed failure never has to put forth any effort at anything, the angry hard-ass doesn't have to take responsibility for the pain he causes in others and so on."

"It's the same with every stupid story we live out. It might be killing us and making us miserable but we generally won't change it because of these three factors."

"So, in order to succeed in changing your story, what I want you to do, is to take some time and write down that stupid story. Describe that defeated and disempowered character. Record the limiting beliefs and all the 'I can'ts' and 'I don'ts.' Write down what secondary benefit you are getting out of that story. Go ahead and take some time to do that," Corey said tossing me a notebook and pen.

I sat on a large boulder in the sun and began to write. I watched as the pen flew across the page, lines and lines of ink spinning out of it, until one page was covered, then two, and then more. It just kept flowing out of me, all these negative ideas and limiting beliefs: "I'm so hurt, she was mean to me, it's not fair my marriage ended, it's not right that our family looks different from the family I grew up in, I'll never find love again, I failed, I should have tried harder, I should have done better, Tim wasn't supposed to die, Bart wasn't supposed to die, I will always feel like this, nothing will ever change, the most important people in my life always die or leave me..."

On and on, I kept writing, covering the pages with black ink. Tears were now streaming down my face and dropping onto the pages, smearing ink where they landed. I couldn't believe there was so much negativity, hurt, anger and doubt inside me.

I kept writing. He kept waiting. And I wrote more.

"God this hurts." I said, looking up from the notebook, finally.

Corey stopped skipping stones and walked over to me from the water's edge. "Your God Damned right it hurts. Now, how often are you telling yourself this story? How many times a day are you repeating this woe-is-me shit in your head?"

"I don't know Corey, it kind of feels like all the time. I call them resentment tapes. They are like a constant argument on audio-tape running in my head."

"All day long, then, C? How many hours a day are you playing this shit in your head?"

"I guess probably at least a couple hours each day, for sure."

"Okay, so let's calculate that out C. You spend two hours each day making yourself feel like shit. There are 365 days in a year and you are 40, so let's say you live another 50 years. That adds up to 36,500 hours. That's over 4 fucking years man. So, you are telling me that you plan to make yourself feel like shit for 4 fucking years. That's your plan, huh? Does that sound like a good idea to you?"

"Well, no," I laughed. "Not when you put it like that."

"Yeah, it sounds like a really fucking stupid plan to me too," he chided me, laughing. "First, I'll teach you how to change your story, how to stop doing that and next, how to fill all those thousands of hours with something better, something that will make you feel good. Now how does that sound for a plan?"

"Much better," I replied.

"Now to change your story: First, go back to each negative element and write it's opposite. 'I'm broken hearted' can become 'My heart is free from getting hurt again.' 'I'm lonely' becomes 'I have space in my life to find true love.' And then, go ahead and burn that paper and lovingly let all of that shit go."

It took a long time—hours I think—to go back through those pages and write out a counter to each sentence. I lost myself in the work, unaware of Corey for a while as I watched my pen move across the white page trailing black ink behind it. My mind was a blur of remembered past and imagined future—each phrase was a small step—one foot in front of the other—one belief, one hurt at a time—and I could feel the shifts starting to happen, the internal movement beginning.

Eventually I looked up from the page and Corey was there patiently waiting. "Great work C, just let that shit go. We're not done yet, though. You see once you get rid of a bad habit in life—like a drug addiction or telling yourself a stupid shitty story—you have to replace it with something else. You have to fill the void with something you want or something you don't want might fill the space."

"This is called *The Universal Law of the Vacuum*. The universe hates empty space and fills it fast."

"Did you ever notice you don't have any empty drawers in your kitchen or desk? Did you ever notice it doesn't matter how small or big your suitcase you will still fill it?"

"The same law holds true here: No empty space. *The Law of the Vacuum.*"

"So, once you get rid of a bad habit or old story, you need to immediately replace it with a good one."

"Now, it's time to write that better story: Let your imagination go, return to that practice which is perfected by children everywhere: daydreaming. Remember how you used to sit in class and stare out the window daydreaming?"

"There were no limits! Anything was possible. You could imagine yourself being a hero, a spy, a famous actor, martial artist, author, anything. Return to that practice and feeling once again. Let your mind wander in the infinite possibilities of stories in the universe, until you find the story you are most attracted to."

"Imagine into the future, feel that creative god-like force flowing through you and let yourself go into what you want to have and do and who you want to be. Imagine the details of the story, where it takes place, what your role in it is, who is included in it with you and so on."

"You see, the old story, the negative self-defeating one was focused on your past. Your new story, the positive empowering and pleasurable one is focused on your present and future."

"It's like when you are driving down the highway in a car. You can't stare in the rear-view mirror all the time or you are going to get in a wreck (plus you'll miss a lot of nice scenery). You have to keep your eyes focused forward, on where you are going."

"It's not where you come from that matters, it's where you are going to."

"So you have got to focus forward, imagine into the future and every now and then, just to check the past, you can glance in that rear-view mirror to learn a lesson or see where you were, but then, right away, you have to return your focus forward, onward into the future you are creating."

"Remember C, you are an American, not an American't. You are a master of Tae Kwon Do, not Tae Kwon Don't!"

"The answer is in the language. So, start to make the story come true. Start by writing it down. When would now be a good time to start?"

With Corey's question still hanging in the air, I suddenly found myself sitting in my office chair staring at my computer screen. A blank document was open and at the top of the page the following words were written:

My Story

The story of my life, from this day forward, without limits, is a story about ...

As I stared at the flashing cursor, I could hear Corey's voice in my mind. "Now, you fill in the rest with your story, with who you are, what you're doing and so on. Let your pen keep moving, your fingers keep typing, don't edit out anything, don't worry if things contradict themselves or you don't know how it would be possible, just write your story down. Use the present or past tense, even for and especially for, things in the future that have not yet happened in your story."

I felt my fingers moving as I watched the words appear on the screen: For example, here is the beginning of the story I am writing about myself and what I have accomplished, and I wrote it on April 26, 2013 (three years before the book was published, when it was just in the earliest stages of conception, in fact).

I am the author of the best-selling book The Art of Becoming: Quantum Leaping into Your Future Self *which has helped millions improve their lives. I am touring and speaking and teaching large groups of people what I have learned. I have a thriving coaching practice, MindBody Mastery Coaching, and am finding fulfillment and purpose in helping others. I am joyfully and completely in love again with a partner perfectly suited to me...*

Again I heard Corey's voice: "Write your story down in as much detail as you can. Allow yourself to feel the emotions you would feel as you write about each wonderful thing you will be, do and have."

I continued typing, the words pouring out even faster than before. I was flying, running away with it as my fingers danced and flittered across the keyboard like a classical pianist.

And in no time, or a few hours, it was finished, written in the present tense and it was amazingly attractive and alluring to me. But, I knew, or thought I knew, at the time that it was nothing more than a bunch of digital lines in a word document, not even ink on a page yet. It wasn't physically real in the world yet.

"You are wondering C. How do I make this story real?" Corey whispered in my mind. "You are thinking you won't truly be happy until that story is real in the physical world. And in answer, I would have to ask you, how did you make the story you are living now real?"

"It may be a difficult question for you to answer. It is for most people because most folks, including you some of the time, have the process of creation reversed in your minds. You see, most people think that their story, the one they tell, is a product of their life. They don't realize that their life is a product of the story they tell."

"Unfortunately, most people think that their emotions are created by external circumstances. They think 'If I could only have _____ I would be happy,' or 'If he or she wouldn't do _____ I would be happy.' So, they go after the thing they think they want, hoping it will produce the feeling they want. But, reality, creation, the law of attraction doesn't work that way."

"It is, instead, the internal energy, the thought, the emotion that creates and attracts the external circumstance or thing. Instead of chasing after the thing, go for the feeling first."

"Thoughts create feelings, and feelings create experiences. Remember that C. Thought-Feeling-Experience. Always in that order."

"When you have a thought about what you want, focus on the feeling first, align with it and the external thing, experience or person will be attracted to you and you to it."

"In addition to being powerful attractors, like magical magnets C, our feelings are the fuel that motivates us to act. It takes emotion to put us into motion. So, in order to align with your story, in order to be what you want to become, in order to turn your intentions into actions and your desires into deeds, you have to create the emotional fuel to get you there."

His voice echoed in my mind, replaying on a looped pattern, again and again, so often that soon it became difficult to distinguish it from my own.

"But just because the process of manifesting anything you want is simple—Thought-Feeling-Experience—doesn't mean it's necessarily going to be easy. Especially if it's important. Especially if you really want it. If it means something to you, you just might have to fight for it, strive for it, live and die for it," I remember him chanting.

As both Corey and Tae Kwon Do competition taught me, you've got to get hungry for it. You've got to want it bad. You have got to want to succeed, to fulfill that dream, that ambition, more than anything. You have got to want it more than you want to sleep. You have got to want it more than you want to play and party. As Eric Thomas so famously says "You have got to want it more than you want to breathe."

There is this story about a body-building champion and how he got started on his successful career. It is said that when he was first starting out he went down to the outdoor gym at muscle beach where all the best body-builders at the time trained and picked out the biggest and best guy there and asked him to train him.

As the story goes the older and larger body-builder said "If you want me to train you, come here." And then he walked out of the gym, across the beach and started walking out in the water.

The younger man followed, until they were about knee deep and asked, "hey, what are we doing, man?"

"Just come on out here," The older body-builder replied until they were both chest deep in the water, waves breaking around their faces.

Then, the much larger and stronger body-builder grabbed the young man by the neck and held his head under water. The young man fought and struggled for all he was worth, dying to get a breath. He panicked and fought even harder, wanting nothing, nothing more than to take just one breath.

Then finally the old man jerked his head out of the water and as he gasped and choked and finally took that breath, the old man asked him: "Will you fight that hard every lift, of every set, every day? Will you put that much effort into everything I tell you to do? Do you want to be a champion even more than you just wanted to breathe? If not, I won't train you."

You have to believe in yourself and your story enough to strive with that kind of intensity.

You have to believe that it's possible.

You have to believe that you deserve it. You have to believe that it's worthwhile. You have to believe that you will succeed.

And when you believe strong enough, when you are focused enough on your goal with such intensity that you can see nothing else, with so much desire that you can think of nothing else, then you will Be it. Every second of every day you will Be it, and that's how you will Become it.

I learned about this kind of focus, this level of intensity, from the years of training and struggle it took me to become a national champion. In my house and Tae Kwon Do school alone (not counting my folks' house or other academies) there are over 50 First Place Trophies or Gold Medals and over 100 more in Second and Third Place Trophies, Silvers and Bronzes. Since each trophy takes several—3 to 7—fights to win, you can calculate over one to three hundred wins without any losses, and several hundred other wins, with only a few losses, in that collection alone.

Of course, that collection doesn't record all the tournaments I went to in the early years, where I never even placed, where I lost and learned, time and time again, because I didn't start out on top.

I had to work my way up over the years, just to reach third place.

The truth is, of course, like most important things I had to push through a lot of pain to find that pleasure. I had to persevere through breakdowns to have my breakthrough. I had to persist through failure before I could exist in success. In fact, there would be a whole lot more second and third place trophies of mine on display, except one night in a fit of rage I threw them all away.

You see, for years I was a good competitor, but never a champion. I would often place first or second in form competitions, and third or even second in fighting, but I never seemed to pull off that first place and title of fighting champion. In fact, my good friend and training partner, who later became the heavy weight world kickboxing champion, Mark Selbee used to call me "second place" as a private nickname, as a joke and a way of motivating me to train and fight harder.

I wanted so desperately to be a champion, to be first place, that I remember coming home one night, very late, after training, and going through my house and collecting every trophy and medal that wasn't first place. I took them all outside and broke each one and threw them all away in a dumpster in the alley. Never again would I settle for less than the best, never again would I accept anything but victory. And it was that day, on that very night, that I began to live and train and eat and sleep like a champion and I have been one ever since.

Whatever it is that you want in life, whatever your dream is, you have to become unwavering, uncompromising, completely obsessed about it. It doesn't matter if your dream is becoming a Tae Kwon Do champion or getting a Ph.D. and becoming a tenured professor and published author or learning wilderness survival and spending months in the backcountry camping and working or opening a Tae Kwon Do school or starting your own business or raising a family (all of which I have done) it doesn't matter what your dream is, or if your dream changes.

What matters is whether or not you achieve and get to live your dream.

All you have to do is become crazy about it. Become obsessed about the What and the Why and the How will show up all by itself. It will show itself to you, naturally and without effort.

I was crazy about Tae Kwon Do, for example. It was my What and my Why. For many years, that's all I thought about, read about, wrote about, practiced, watched, talked about, trained for, cross-trained for, lived for.

It's funny and perhaps a bit hard to believe but there were many years of my life that are straight out of a 1980's martial arts movie.

Yes, I lived in a little house behind my Martial Arts Master. Yes, my roommate was also a Martial Arts student, master and best friend. Yes, we taught and trained together and read and discussed books on philosophy, martial arts, anatomy and much more.

Yes, our Master's wife fed us traditional food, kimchi and bulgolgi. Yes, for the first year, living the monastic martial art life in that small house, we didn't have running water and carried our drinking water in by hand and went outside with a shovel into the woods or out on the prairie, even in winter, to go to the bathroom.

And yes, we did break through the ice on the pond in winter and jump in and run barefoot through the snow and train in the sun and 100 degree heat and humidity and have big bonfires at night and break flaming logs with our feet and hands. Yes, we did all of that…and more.

I remember during this period of time that each night I would come home from Tae Kwon Do and go kneel in my room over a cinder block on which there was an old Tae Kwon Do uniform folded up. For about 10 to 15 minutes every night, I would sit there kneeling and punching that block, body forging my knuckles and fists, bleeding on the uniform again and again until it was blackish brown from incessant blood stains. Thump. Thump. Thump. Thump. Again and again, each bone shaking thump, thickening the layers of bone, increasing the density and strength of the trabeculae, the walls of hollow bone, as the skin hardened and callused, until that fist could punch through anything.

I can recall so many crazy things we did, playing so seriously with our practice, devising so many ways to test and improve ourselves: like practicing punching and kicking out a candle flame without knocking the candle over to improve both speed and control. Or the cinder block we hooked up on a rope and pulley outside under the tree, so we could hoist the block up and drop it onto our stomachs in order to body forge the abdomen for taking hits during fighting and for board break demonstrations over the abdomen.

Was all of that or any of it really necessary? Of course not, but if you want to succeed at anything, if you want to become anything, you have to get obsessive about it. There are times when being obsessive and compulsive is a useful strategy and when we are talking about achieving a dream, especially one that takes work, this is one of those times.

I had already learned in those days the power of motivating yourself and by bringing me back to those times and by adding some new teachings, Corey showed me four ways to feel the truth and power of my story, to align with it and get so hungry for it that I could attract it, and everything in it, to me.

First Corey taught me to write out an affirmation or incantation, just like those described in chapter four that summarized my life story. And each day I would recite this powerful spell, retell myself this positive story, until I started to believe it. And once I started believing it of course I started being it, until I finally achieved it.

Second, "each day, at least once per day," he said "do your basic relaxation meditation and visualize yourself in your new story." He told me that you should see yourself in the story as if you are watching it on a movie screen. Listen to the sounds, watch what you are doing and how you are acting. Then merge with yourself so that you can see the scene from within the eyes of your visualized self, the new self. Go through the new story and enjoy it, as if it were a daydream, from within the perspective of your new self. Do this each day.

Third, create a vision card with pictures and words that represents your new story. It can be any size. Make sure it has images and phrases of the things you want to be, do and have in your story. Put it up where you can see it every day. And take some time to look at it each day and to feel the wonderful feelings of already having and being and doing all of those things you desire.

And finally, as ideas come to you write about them. Keep a journal to start recording things that you could do to start making that new story happen. Many might seem obvious to you at first and you might create a fairly long list quickly that looks like obstacles: "I need to save money to go back to college, but I can't." Don't worry about the things on the list that look like obstacles. In fact, don't worry about doing anything on the list unless you feel inspired to do it. Wait for other weird, inspired ideas to come to you, like I could just apply for some online editing jobs and see what happens or I could take one of those free online classes I heard about, etc. Create task lists, steps that will move you in the direction of your goal.

And when the four practices listed above get you all fired up and passionate and motivated about your dream, start taking those steps toward your goal. And each day take another step forward and another and keep on going, putting one foot in front of the other, until you look up and find you are already living deep inside your story and the life of your dreams.

I once saw taped to a wall in Corey's office, a haiku scrawled on a page in black magic marker that read:

> Lao Tzu's Teaching on How to Get
> Through Hell and Into Heaven
> Put one foot in front
> Of the other, and each day,
> Take one step, forward.

I am literally living out this story, right now in my life. I mean it. Literally. Sometimes I write things down in here in this story and *then* later I live them. They happen in my life, in reality, after they have been written down in this story. And of course there are also things that happen in my life first that I then, later write down in this story.

It is an eerie experience, much like a cross between de ja vu and telekinesis and precognition, all wrapped up in one. At one and the same time I am feeling the future, predicting it, affecting and directing it and noticing how familiar it is, how much I remember it, from long, long before…. It is difficult to explain and extremely powerful to experience. When you begin doing this work, when you begin really experiencing it in your life, you will feel incredible, magical, all powerful. You will feel like it doesn't matter in any way what happens because you can handle it, you can change it and create any thing, any experience, any one, you want.

Either way you look at it, I am living out a story right now. In fact the reason I wrote this book, *The Art of Becoming,* was because it is the story of what I wanted my life to Be and now it is the story of what my life has Become.

The cause and effect demand each other, both happen, both move toward each other. In a way cause and effect happen simultaneously. Or you could say at times, things in your story cause the same things to happen in your life, while at other times things in your life cause the same things to happen in your story.

Whether you are conscious of it or not, you are writing your own life story and then living it, in the same exact manner that I am, did and continue to do. However I am very aware, conscious and in control of the story I am writing, and thus the one I am living.

How about you?

You can choose your story or have it chosen for you. Period.

Are you living out a story that was written by conscious design of your own or by default? Are you living by intention or accident? Are you writing your own story or have you let others write it for you?

If you could write a different story for your life, would you?

If so what would it be?

Write out the heroic story of your past and all that you have gone through and done and learned and experienced and felt to get here now.

And then write out the great story and joyful purpose ahead of you—the amazing and wonderful things you will be, and have and do and feel.

What character are you?

What are your great challenges and triumphs? What is your purpose, your trajectory, the plotline of your life? What are your special strengths and traits? Who are your allies?

What is your special destiny? What is your quest and what do you need to find? Why do you know you will succeed?

Who will help you along the way and who will enjoy your triumphs with you?

What will you learn along the way? And who will you become?

When you imagine the story of your life, when you dream make sure that you DREAM BIG!

Write it now, your story without limits and Right now even as you think about it, you are beginning to live it.

You are breathing life into that story dear reader with each breath, with each thought and each feeling. Feel your story coming to life until you are living it now.

You, dear reader, already are and have been living the life and story of your dreams!

CHAPTER SEVEN

HOW TO BE ANYTHING

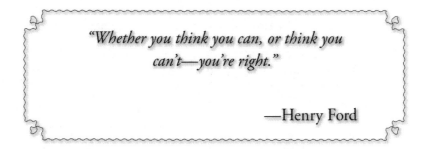

"Whether you think you can, or think you can't—you're right."

—Henry Ford

When I landed next to Corey on this particular leap, we were at my parent's house in Kansas and for some reason we were standing on the pitched, wood-shingled roof.

"It's a little windy! Watch your footing there!" Corey yelled at me striving to be heard over the gusting Kansa, or south-wind.

"Why are we here?" I asked.

In reply Corey just pointed off to my side, where I suddenly became aware of my younger self, standing next to a large hang glider with a motorcycle helmet on my head. Instantly I knew why we were here and I let myself drift right back into the moment.

I watched and remembered all those years ago, standing high up on the roof of the family house, the wind whistling through my ears as visions of flight danced through my head. I hauled on a thick rope, slowly pulling my latest invention up the side of the house. I was always making inventions in those days, always involved in some sort of scheme to make my latest dream come true. Some of these projects ended in success and quite often they ended in spectacular failures.

I was not alone however, in these failures. In fact we are always in good company, when we fail. Thomas Edison, himself, claimed to have failed over a thousand times in his attempts to invent a commercially viable light-bulb. And in 1903, just a few months before the Wright brothers had their first successful flight at Kitty Hawk, *The New York Times* predicted that it would be over a million years before man achieved self-propelled flight.

History shows that our greatest dreams and greatest dreamers are often the only ones who believed their dream was even possible. Even as a small child, especially as a small child I knew this to be true.

As I was preparing for that first test flight, I tried not to think of all the other early aviators whose first flights ended in injury, but I couldn't keep such fear-filled thoughts out of my head. I recalled reading about the Benedictine monk Eilmer of Malmesbury who flew 200 meters in a glider during the 11th century and the Muslim Abbas Ibn Firnas whose first flight was 200 years earlier. Both pilots sustained serious injuries. Neither flew again. "Maybe they flew from higher up than I'm going to" I thought, trying to console myself that I would survive this first flight and build my confidence up for the jump.

I remember knowing better than to look down, over the edge and instead kept my focus fixed firmly on the glider in front of me. Crawling under the bamboo and plastic glider, I clipped myself into a makeshift harness and raised the awkward contraption up onto my shoulders. Standing finally, I grabbed the crossbar of the steering mechanism, touched the barn owl feathers that were tied there for good luck and turned to face the wind.

A strong southerly wind swept across the plains, rolled up the hill and shot over the house. I could feel it pushing me back, thrusting on the glider which even now was billowing like a sail on a ship. Fear settled in my stomach like a rock and doubt weighed me down. But, there was nothing left to do, save jump.

I had dreamt of this moment for months. I had lain awake in bed countless nights flying over fields and forests in my mind. I had watched the soaring flight of birds, studied the circling of vultures and the shapes of wings. I had read books, learned the history of aviation, and carefully studied a variety of flying machines and blueprints for modern hang gliders.

In class, when I was supposed to be memorizing the names of the presidents, I gazed out the window, daydreaming of flight. I imagined it was 2,000 years earlier in China and I was Yuan Huangtou, the imprisoned son of the emperor, escaping his brick walls by tying himself to a large, home-made kite. I filled my notebooks at school with detailed drawings, with replicas and revisions of Leonardo Da Vinci's 15th century sketches of self-propelled flying machines. And I studied the writings of Swedenborg and Cayley, learning the basics behind the physics of lift, drag and angle of attack.

I had climbed tall trees to linger in their uppermost branches, gazing at the canopy of the forests around my home as if I were flying over them. I was obsessed with the dream of flight, the elusive freedom of taking to the air, the vision that had shadowed men from above for ages. I could not climb back down now. This I knew. The only way back to the ground, the only way to sanity and contented sleep was to jump over the edge.

I began walking, then awkwardly running, toward the edge where the roof ended abruptly and only the wind and the long distance down to the ground remained. As I stumbled forward, the wind howled louder in my ears and the plastic sheeting of the kite popped and snapped around me like thunder. The noise in my ears was deafening, until I came to the edge and launched myself out, into the void.

Suddenly, it was as if everything stopped.

I no longer heard the billowing wind or the fluttering of the glider's plastic wings. They filled like a sail, stretched tight and curved up into a perfect airfoil. I felt myself rising and gaining lift.

If my mind wasn't already filled with pure ecstasy, I would have thought about Bernoulli's Principle of aerodynamics, how the air slowed underneath the wing, deflecting it upward and creating lift. But at that moment, I couldn't think at all; my mind was as blank as the blue sky, full of nothing but pure, wordless joy. I was hanging motionless in the air, about twenty feet from the house. More importantly, however, I was now ten feet higher than the roof.

The joy of a dream no longer deferred filled me. It lifted me as gracefully as the wind lifted the glider. "I'm flying!" I thought, the words finally forming in my mind. And then, the kite folded like an umbrella.

I awoke on the ground, my mouth filled with dirt, my body aching, ankle on fire and mind hazy with confusion. I lay still for a few moments, trying to catch my breath and collect my thoughts.

"Yes, I was on the ground. Yes, I had flown… Ah, yes," I remember thinking finally, "the bamboo struts must have broken." I checked the glider over carefully, while still lying on the ground, since I did not think I could stand yet. The bamboo struts were indeed broken. They had not held up under the weight and the pressure. But I had, if only for a moment, flown.

"And after that big old kite folded up and dumped you in the dirt C, did you give up? Did you consider that first flight a failure C?" Corey asked.

"No. Of course not." I replied. "It was a massive success, and a critical learning experience. I hauled that wreckage back to the barn and replaced the bamboo struts with aluminum piping and climbed right back out onto that roof and jumped again..."

"That's right C. When you fall down, *you don't give up, you get up.* Make that a maxim for your life. And turn failure into feedback and problems into opportunities to learn and you can achieve anything."

"It's not the size of the dream that matters. It's how much energy you put into it. And that energy all starts with belief."

"If you want to achieve anything, if you want to manifest anything, you have got to believe it first: believe it to achieve it."

"And that C, is precisely why I brought you back here to Kansas on this windy day. I want you to put this little mantra in your memory bank:"

"If you can conceive it, you can believe it. And if you can believe it, you can achieve it."

"I can tell you from personal experience and long practice C, that you can achieve anything, you can be, have and do anything."

"You see, many of us end up living lives that are not fulfilling, not the lives of our fullest potential because we end up believing in the limits that others have programmed into us, limitations based upon their own fears, from society, the media, peers, parents and so on."

"For example, I'm sure most of us believe the story that achieving flight was hard for humans. Most readers probably believe that ordinary folks like you and me don't make hang gliders and fly them, that this is reserved for specialists, with training and special equipment and so on. You, dear reader, have probably never built a hang glider or never tried to fly or never built your own submarine or climbed a mountain, not because you didn't want to, but because you didn't think that it was possible for you."

"I want this to be absolutely clear to you C, you built and launched and flew your own hang glider simply because you wanted to and most importantly because you believed you could. This is how we do anything, how we achieve anything, how we become anything. First we believe, then we achieve."

"Unfortunately many people go through life 'being' people they don't want to be, and 'achieving' things they don't want to achieve, because they have been programmed to believe in the wrong things. Many people have been programmed to believe things like 'I'm fat. I'm ugly. I'm awkward. I'm angry. I'm alone. I'm a druggy. I'm a whore. I'm stupid. I'm no good at math. I'll never amount to anything. The odds are stacked against me. I'm supposed to be an accountant because I'm good at math. I shouldn't leave my husband or my secure job. I'm good with my hands but not smart enough for college.'"

"The truth is C, we all have limiting beliefs like these, stories we don't need to tell ourselves, stories that do us no good. And although they seem powerful and convincing to us, although they often feel like facts, they are just stories, just beliefs. They are nothing more than fictions we have made up. And they can be changed just as easily."

"We have no limits but those that are programmed into us. No limits but those we set for ourselves. As Richard Bach wrote "Argue for your limitations and sure enough they're yours.""

"For example C, if you had asked anyone what they thought of your plan to build and fly a hang glider all by yourself, what do you think they would have said?"

"Well that's true, I didn't ask anyone or even tell anyone, I just did it. If I had asked anyone though, they would have most definitely said it was impossible. Now, not my parents or Bart, they would have said it was impossible for most people but would have told me to go for it and well, mom would have said to be careful too. But, other than them, most folks would have believed it was impossible and that I'd never do it." I replied.

"Exactly C. For them, for those disbelievers, of course it was impossible, but not because they didn't have the knowledge or skill—You didn't have any special knowledge of aerodynamics or engineering skills. It was impossible for them because they believed it was impossible."

"You can only achieve that which you believe. It is the belief that creates the possibility."

"In much the same way that many people used to think flight was impossible in 1954 the prevailing belief was that it was impossible for a human being to run a mile in under 4 minutes. Everyone believed this because it had been tried again and again and no one had ever run the mile in less than 4 minutes. The belief in medical, scientific and athletic communities, the prevailing belief of every expert at the time was supported by thousands of trials all of which seemed to prove that the 4 minute mile was physically impossible."

"Then Roger Banister came along and not only did he break the 4 minute mile barrier, he crushed it. Once it had been accomplished one time, once it had been proven possible, everyone's beliefs about it changed. And since that time, since everyone's beliefs changed, over 20,000 people have broken the 4 minute mile barrier including kids in high school."

"What do you think changed C? Are we to believe that the athletes of today, even high school athletes are physically different from and are that much better than the best athletes and Olympians of the past. What is more likely that the human body and it's physical capabilities changed, that they permanently evolved for thousands of people in just a few moments or that once people's beliefs changed their abilities changed?"

"As soon as other athletes saw that a 4 minute mile was possible, as soon as they began to believe in it, then they began to achieve it. This illustrates the powerful principal that we must first believe before we can achieve."

"Believe that you can and you will. Believe that you already are and you will become."

I found myself at home, coming out of a trance with those words echoing through my mind and then, as if from just behind my right ear, I heard Corey in the faintest of whispers say a single name: "Hellen Keller."

Of course, I was very familiar with her amazing story, but I did some research on her life story anyway, just to see what might show up and why Corey had whispered her name to me. Hellen was born with the ability to see and hear but at 19 months she contracted an illness that left her both deaf and blind. It was believed by many that Helen was incapable of learning that she would never learn to communicate or interact fully with others and that it would be impossible for her to have any sort of a normal life.

However after much searching her parents were lucky enough to find Hellen's first teacher, Anne Sullivan. Anne herself was a visually impaired teacher at, and former student of, the Perkin's Institute for the Blind. And because Anne believed in her and so persistently refused to accept her supposed limitations, Hellen Keller overcame the greatest of obstacles. She not only learned to speak, but also to write, earned her Bachelor's Degree and went on to publish twelve books and to give lectures at colleges and universities across the country.

As I read more about her, the familiar story took on a much more incredible meaning for me. I began to think about what I believed was possible and impossible for me a little bit differently. And as I read further I found this wonderful gem: One of her teachers, Sir Everett Hale, wrote the following poem about her and about the power each individual has over his or her own life and the world; it is called "I am only one"

I am only one

I can't do everything

But still I am one

I can do something

And because I cannot do everything

I will not refuse to do

That one thing which I can do

Too many people, too much of the time, refuse to do what they can or want to do, simply because they don't believe it is possible for them.

What is it that you want to do, dear reader? What is it that you dream of doing, but you think is impossible?

What obstacles do you face? Are they bigger than Hellen Keller's or are they smaller and if she can overcome hers, why can't you overcome yours?

For many people, the title of this chapter would make more sense if it read "How to Become Anything." But, I have titled it, as I have—"How to Be Anything"—for a very specific reason: One of the main reasons people do not become what, or who, they want to be is because of a very powerful trick played on us by the semantics of our language.

In addition to the limiting beliefs that we have programmed into us, the very structure of our language and how we perceive reality severely limits what we believe we can be or become. The concept of Linguistic Relativity that the language we speak shapes and affects how we see the world in many powerful ways is most notably linked to the work of Benjamin Whorf and Edward Sapir.

A classic example that is often used to explain the Sapir-Whorf hypothesis is to compare the Inuit words for and perceptions of snow with those of English speakers. In English we have only one primary word for snow, but we do have some variations that can be used and some other words that can be added to describe the different types or qualities of snow. We can, for example, distinguish between slushy snow and powdery snow or between snowflakes and snowdrifts.

In Inuktitut on the other hand, there are many more words for snow, many more variations of the word in their language to describe the many different types of snow in their environment. Because of their language Inuit's can distinguish between more types of snow than English speakers. They can actually see differences in between types of snow that we cannot see or distinguish, much less speak about.

Their entire perception and their actual experience of their frozen world, is different than ours. One major difference for example, is that we don't even recognize or experience much of what they do in their environment because we lack the language for it. Arctic travelers and those who have lived with the Inuit have historically either adopted the native terms for snow, when there were no English counterparts, or have been forced to create new words in English to match the Inuit terms. In order to function effectively in Arctic environments, English speakers have had to change their language so that they are no longer bound by its limits.

Language influences our perceptions of how we "become" something in much the same way. In the English language, it is accepted that "become" is before "be." Both the logic of our language, its syntax or word order and how we define those words dictates that one must *Become* something before he or she can *Be* it. We are told that we must move through *Becoming* before we arrive at *Being.*

But this is not how reality works.

As I finished typing those words I heard a faint whisper from somewhere behind me in the room. His voice, tiptoeing on the wind:

"In reality, in order to Become anything, you must first Be it C. This is called *The Universal Law of Being and Becoming.* This Law states that before you can Become something, you have to Be it first."

"Before you can Become a success you have to Be one in your thoughts and actions. Before you can Become a straight 'A' student, you have to Be one every day when you study. Before you can Become a published author, you have to Be a writer on a daily basis."

I suppose this might have been when time started to get really fuzzy for me. It must have started slowly and gradually built up until I finally noticed it, so it's hard to tell when it began. But time sort of started slipping or getting confused for me.

As I grew closer and closer to Corey, I started having conversations with him even when I wasn't quantum leaping. And it seemed like sometimes I was quantum leaping to him without meditating, like during the middle of my day. We were becoming so "entangled" in the terms of Quantum Physics that merely thinking about him would leap me to him or him to me or both of us somewhere else.

So there I was a few days later, walking across campus on a drizzly and dark Friday morning, still working at the University and on my way to teach class. The rain splattered softly in tiny droplets and mist as it fell. All the people around me walked down the wet sidewalks and across the puddled streets with their heads hunkered down, lost in their own worlds.

As I turned up a heavily tree-lined walkway his voice was once again inside my head.

"We learn by doing, you know. Everyone is familiar with this. But I prefer to say it this way: We Become by Being."

"It is the same recognition but more powerfully articulated and it leads to some important recognitions. You see we cannot become who or what we want to be by remaining what we are. Most people however, are too rooted in what they are, too attached to it; they spend too much time thinking about who they are now, too much emotional attachment and ego tied into who they are now and not enough time thinking about who they want to be. The more you think about and notice who you are now, the more you stay the same. The more you think about and notice who you want to be, the more you become it."

"But here is the catch, the place where most people get hung up. They have the logic reversed. They know what they want to be so they try to become it, thinking of becoming as a gradual process of transition and incremental change. They think I will spend some time becoming it then eventually I will be it. This however, is not how the universe and the law of attraction and the process of growth work. *The Universal Law of Being and Becoming* states that if you want to Become something, you have to Be it."

"You do not have to wait. Now is the moment to step into your future self. Be it now. Feel it now. Live it now. Be it now for yourself and you will Become it later for others."

By this point on the walk to my office, I was climbing a set of stairs, at the top of which it was my habit to turn around and look at Humboldt Bay for a few minutes while saying gratitudes. As I habitually turned and looked across the gray waters mirrored by equally gray clouds above, I suddenly felt my arms shoot up over my head of their own accord, fists pumping in a victory pose. I saw a brief flash in my mind of Rocky Balboa jogging in place, fists uplifted at the top of gray stairs and then I felt the lightning strike of kundalini energy surging up my spine and I felt my whole body and the back of my skull tingling.

And suddenly, I was no longer standing at the top of the stairs at Humboldt State University looking out at the bay. Instead I was high above the University of Kansas's massive Memorial Stadium at the foot of the WWII Memorial Camponile. The massive tower soared above me and chimed the top of the hour. A robin sang and whistled from a good sized oak on my left and the long grassy hill rolled out before and below me. The stadium lay down below, opened up like an oyster with thousands of stadium seats rising up and out like wings.

As I sat and took in the scene, I remembered that I had been there before, for the 1988 Junior Olympics. As I looked down the hill a second time during my quantum leap, I suddenly saw the long lines of athletes stretched out and snaking around the campus's many sidewalks. Team after team, after countless other teams, stood waiting to follow the torch into the stadium for the opening ceremonies. Thousands of them.

I remember being there: I had just turned 16, it was my biggest Tae Kwon Do competition yet and I was scared. I remember breaking my right arm early in my last match and despite finishing the fight, I couldn't pull off a one-armed win. I took home a bronze and I met—and lost to and broke my arm against—one of the toughest fighters I would ever face. For years we would maintain a respectful rivalry of always training to beat each other at the next tournament. Eight years later, I would finally beat him.

As I sat there at the foot of the Camponile memorial, I could actually see where the Kansas teams were standing and I got to witness a wonderful scene of my teenage self in action. A bunch of us from the Tae Kwon Do team were standing in line talking with athletes from the state track team. As soon as they heard we were the "karate guys" the typical conversation ensued:

"Does that stuff really work?" One guy asked. "Show us something." Another challenged.

And as usual, we all replied "yes it does work" and "no we didn't feel like showing off anything." The standard reply.

After a bit of this back and forth, the largest guy on their team, who towered over me at well over 6 foot tall, said "Well, I don't care about that karate crap, anyway."

This statement had always been one that pissed me off and one that offered such an invitation I just couldn't pass it up. So without saying a word, I did a jump spinning round kick—a flying spinning move that turns the body 360 degrees in an impressive and gymnastic motion—and I smacked the bill of his baseball cap with my foot, spinning the entire hat around backwards on his head without even hurting him. At the same moment, I let out an ear splitting, deafening and frightening Ki-yap, a roar the likes of which the non-martial arts athletes had never heard before. Jaws dropped faster than I landed on the ground.

And then I heard myself saying, loud enough for both teams to hear "You care now, don't you?" At first, there was silence, then laughter and cheering from both teams.

As I watched my younger self and the scene unfold, I thought back to how finally, after years of working and getting only the same mediocre results, I became a true champion.

Although I was a good competitor and I had made it to the Junior Olympics, I consistently took second and third place for many years in competitions. I could not seem to break that champion barrier and win first place consistently. This struggle went on for almost a decade.

"That's why I brought you here C." Corey said, breaking into my reverie. "I want to make sure you see clearly that you realize how you became a champion, so you can help others be and become what they most want to be. Regardless of the goal C, the process is always the same. This is the great secret of how to become anything."

"You must Be it to Become it."

"This is what you did in your twenties. This is how you finally became a champion. Now," Corey said, "Let's take another leap. I want you to see how you became a champion"

Corey grabbed my arm and we leaped. Immediately I found myself transported in time and space to Manhattan Kansas in the mid 1990's. It was dark and quiet. We were sitting in what looked like an old roman coliseum, the limestone steps of the old unused football stadium surrounded the outdoor track and field, while the stars shown down from above.

Down below on the track a lone figure was running interval wind sprints. He sprinted past our side of the coliseum, legs and arms pumping furiously, breath coming in strong and regulated rhythms and in an instant he was gone. Fast. Then, at the end of the straight away his pace slowed into a steadied, disciplined jog, which he maintained at the same pace around the corner, down the straight away on the far side of the track and around second corner, until he came once again to the straight away on our side and then he exploded. A blur of movement. A wind racing past.

"Yes I remember this," I said. "I was doing interval training. Dad and I did a lot of research in those days on the best ways to cross-train for Tae Kwon Do. We discovered that the best cardio-vascular and strength training for athletes like me, for boxers, martial artists and wrestlers was the 1 to 4 sprint-jog ratio studied and developed by the German Olympic teams. Athletes like us need both fast twitch muscle fibers for explosive strength and speed, as well as high cardiovascular endurance. If we jog for endurance however, we will replace our short, explosive muscle fibers with longer slower ones. The best way for us to train in order to gain cardiovascular endurance and maintain our explosive strength is to use intervals in this 1 to 4 ratio. The sprinting maintains explosive strength and speed while using the slow jog interval allows us to maintain our target heart rate for over 30 minutes. This is important because it takes 20 minutes of maintaining your target heart rate to stimulate capillary growth in the muscles. Although few people realize this, there are two components to cardio-vascular endurance: the health and strength of your heart is one and vascularity or the number of capillaries in your muscles is the second."

"Yes Dad helped us a lot. But you did a lot more than just cardio-vascular cross training." Corey said, interrupting my impromptu lecture.

"Oh yes most definitely, I was in the gym, lifting weights for over an hour every morning, 5 days a week for years. And then all the research on sports nutrition. I even gave up my beloved peanut butter and was eating banana mixed with wheat germ on my bagels to reduce fat intake. I was crazy," I said, laughing and remembering the total focus I had at the time.

"Remember your mirror, the countdown clock, and all the affirmations?" Corey said, egging on my reverie, as we watched my 20 year old self continue to race rhythmically around the track.

"Yes, I had a picture of Michael G, the toughest fighter I ever faced and my arch nemesis, on my mirror and underneath it I had a note that said: 'Today Michael G. is having the best training day of his life. What are you doing?'"

"And then on the living room wall there was a huge dry erase board where every day I would write how many training days were left until the next competition. And my truck, that little old Mitsubishi I used to drive, I had pasted all over the steering wheel and dashboard all kinds of affirmations."

"That's right Corey and there are two important points I want you to recognize."

"First, you didn't slowly become a champion. You quite literally, simply and powerfully made a decision to start living like one. In order to Become a champion, you first had to Be one."

"In order to become a champion, you had to start thinking, acting and living like a champion. You had to get up in the morning and eat like a champion and hit the gym like a champion; and you had to eat and re-hydrate all day like a champion and train again in the evening like a champion and meditate like a champion and sleep like a champion, day in and day out."

"And most importantly, in order for you to do all of these things like a champion you had to think and feel like a champion. You had to Be a champion for quite some time for yourself before you could Become one, that is before you could 'Become' one that other people recognized and called champion. You had to feel it first and to believe it before you could become it."

"The second important point to recognize is that once you decided to Be a champion, once you began to think, feel and act like one, it didn't take very long at all until you Became one."

"You trained and competed in Tae Kwon Do for almost 10 years with similar results, lots of second and third places and a few firsts. Then you decided to believe you could be a champion. Then you decided to Be a champion. And in less than a year you were taking first in almost every tournament you attended and you had Become a champion, one who would maintain that winning streak until retiring from competition."

"The key lesson here is that you must feel it first then it will manifest. Whatever it is that you want to achieve, you have to first make yourself feel as if you have already achieved it. You must truly get yourself into the exact same state or emotion you will feel when you have your goal, then you can work on any sort of technique for accomplishing it, whether it is a visualization technique or an exercise program."

"We have to master ourselves before we can master our world. We have to master the inner condition before we can master the outer condition. Do you see what I'm saying C?"

"Yes absolutely. Every thing on the outside came first from the inside." I replied.

"Exactly C, once you mastered your inner condition and you started to believe that you were a champion (not that you could become one, but that you were one), you started to behave like one."

"And Behaving is Being. And Being leads to Becoming."

"To state it as simply as I can, in a single word, the Art of Becoming is Being."

"So remember C: Inner mastery always comes before outer mastery. Inner change always precedes outer change." Corey's voice faded in my mind and I found myself—back home from my leap—standing at the top of the stairs at Humboldt State, staring out at the bay. I turned away from the rain-drenched view of the gray clouds over the bay and continued across campus to class.

As I walked, thinking about the inside and the outside, the following interesting and paradoxical realization occurred to me: the only reason we want to master outer conditions is because we think that it will make our inner conditions better. The only reason we want to achieve anything is because we think it will make us happy. But if we can master our inner conditions and manifest the happiness and fulfillment we are going for anyway, it won't even matter if the outer conditions change. We will already be happy anyway. And of course the outer conditions will change, but that won't even matter much anymore.

One way we might come to understand this process is with the analogy of osmosis. When two solutions are separated by a permeable barrier and we add a whole bunch of salt, for example, to one solution, eventually the salt will cross the barrier and join the other solution. This will continue until there is the same amount of salt dissolved in both solutions, until an equilibrium is reached. The same happens energetically on the Quantum level with our thoughts, emotions and manifested physical reality. When you turn up the emotions inside you, when you concentrate the solution inside you with enough emotion, it flows by osmosis outside of you and manifests in your world.

When you experience this process at work, it will feel completely magical, miraculous, freaky even. You get to have this amazing experience of intentionally changing your inner reality and then watching as it just unfolds in front of you. It is literally the experience of watching your dreams magically manifest into reality.

One very wild experience or series of experiences I had with this, came in the spring of 2013, one year before I would leave my job at Humboldt State University and an 18 year career in higher education. Most people would have said that I was crazy to walk away from a permanent job as a tenured professor with a guaranteed salary and health benefits for a career that existed only in my mind. And I wanted to be sure of it myself, so I was spinning certainty in all kinds of ways to fortify my belief that I could and would immediately become a success in my new career as a life coach, author and personal growth expert.

At that point in my life though, I didn't have a single paying client and this book wasn't even a complete manuscript yet. It didn't make much sense to place all my bets for the future on a career that had not yet physically manifested in any form at all, but that's exactly what I was doing. I was confidently announcing my departure from the University, helping to find a replacement and spinning certainty every day. In a number of different forms, every day I would practice visualizations, incantations, powerful questions and gratitudes, and every day I would feel my faith grow.

During this time, I would consistently feel the physical sensation of floating. When I was driving on the highway for example, I would often viscerally feel the car floating, rising up off the road and coasting on certainty. Or while walking across campus or through my house, I would notice that I could barely feel the floor, that I felt like I was walking on air, flying on faith.

I was building my career, and my confidence and my certainty of success, from the inside out. I was working on it internally even more than externally. I was being my new self before I became it, believing before achieving, and it felt great!

Then as the clients started coming in and their lives changed radically for the better and they referred me to other clients and the pages filled up and the publishers responded enthusiastically, I got to watch it all manifest from belief into being, from my imagination into my reality.

Here are two techniques that you can use to build the kind of unshakeable certainty that will enable you to manifest every thing and any thing you want. The first is a reflective exercise, a written one, and the second is a visualization exercise, a version of what is called in Neuro-Linguistic Programming "a swish" pattern.

First write out your goal, your dream in as much detail as possible, in present tense. Write down what it will feel like to achieve it, what it will look like, sound like, every detail.

And in order to motivate yourself, write down all the good things that will come from succeeding and all the bad consequences of failing.

Then write down all the reasons you know you will succeed. All the examples of others who have succeeded, all the experiences in your past, every resource and ally and supporter you have, write down everything that tells you this is possible.

Then in your meditative state after relaxing and breathing deep down into Alpha, think about something that you are absolutely certain about. It can be something simple like the fact that you are completely certain the sun will rise tomorrow or something specific to yourself, something you are absolutely certain you can do, something that you know for absolute, complete certainty. Notice where the image of this thing is, what color, what shape, whether it is moving or still, whether it has a border or not, how close it is, how big and so on. And notice what sounds you hear, their volume, pitch, what they are, the direction they are coming from, while also noticing the feelings inside your body and which way they are moving and spinning.

Next you will think about your goal, the thing you want to do or be certain about. Call up that image and move it to exactly the same place of your certainty image and make it look like your certainty image exactly, in shape, color, size and so on. Make the sounds associated with your new endeavor sound the same in volume, tempo and direction as your certainty image, and make the feelings spin the same way in your body as you think about your new goal.

Now very quickly, flip back and forth from one image to the other, a bunch of times, while keeping the image in the same place and the feelings of certainty, spinning the same way.

When you are done with both of these exercises you will feel so certain about succeeding at your new endeavor, even if it is walking on water that you won't *try* it; you will simply and powerfully *do* it.

When Corey installed certainty in me about leaving my tenured position at the University to start a private coaching practice he used my dad's death experience. When I was pulling my dad out of the water and seeing with full knowledge what the glazed-over look of death in his eyes meant, I kept hearing a powerful voice of certainty shouting in my mind and I knew, I absolutely knew, despite the facts, despite the CPR rate of failure, despite the reality of the situation in front of me, I knew that I would bring him back.

And when we merged them, the image of me saving my Dad's life with the picture of my new life and career path, I became as certain of professional success in my new career as I was that day of being able to beat even death and I knew then that nothing could deter me, daunt me or hold me back. And nothing has.

When you are absolutely, 100% certain of success, why hold back or hesitate? Wouldn't you joyfully throw yourself into any task whole-heartedly, especially if you knew you were going to win?

That is one of several very powerful truths that I learned that day on the beach watching my father die and come back to life. First I learned that I can do anything I put my energy into without limit, even stop death. Second I learned how to take this same exact sense of powerful certainty, of absolute conviction and unshakeable faith, and put it into any dream, any aspiration.

And equally important, as I stood there looking at my father's lifeless form, while the waves crashed at my feet and the wind howled by like the minutes ticking off the clock, I realized the truth: Most people go to the grave with their best ideas, their greatest aspirations and inventions still inside them, un-manifested in the world. Most people die with their greatest potential not yet realized.

Don't die before you get a chance to sing your song. Don't go to the grave before you get to see your dream come true, manifested in the world, right in front of you.

What dreams, dear reader, what hopes and aspirations, what inspirations and inventions, what ideas live inside you now that you have not yet brought forth into the world?

If you die tomorrow what will you have left undone, unfinished?

What dream will you not even yet have begun?

What ideas are still inside you waiting to get out?

As you think about them write them down. Write them all down.

Now, How far are you willing to go to make them happen? What are you willing to sacrifice to make your greatest purpose and aspirations come true? How long can you commit and persevere to see it through?

Tell me, dear reader, what are you willing to anything do in order to live the life of your dreams?

And when would now be a good time to start?

CHAPTER EIGHT

THE POWER OF PRETEND

> *"Take up one idea. Make that one idea your life--think of it, dream of it, live on that idea. Let the brain, muscles, nerves, every part of your body, be full of that idea, and just leave every other idea alone. This is the way to success."*
>
> —*Swami Vivekananda*

Bart could tell good stories. Bart could tell the best stories.

Often I would do something with him and later would hear him tell someone about it, and although I could barely recognize his version, I liked it much better and would remember it as the real version from then on after.

As Bart always said, "Never let the truth get in the way of a good story."

Life is what you make of it.

And you know the language we use has a lot of power. Whether we are repeating a mantra or incantation or simply speaking to others, our words carry power, emotion, information, energy and impact. Our words cast spells. The secrets are hidden in the language. Why do you think they call it Spelling?

You see what you say, you also feel and hear it, and have to take it in to understand it.

(Did you see that? It's okay if you missed it.)

Then there are those things you say all the time. You don't realize that you are repeating them daily, like a spell or mantra or incantation, but you are.

For example, how do you typically respond when someone says, "Hello, how are you?"

You know that your response is almost always the same. What is it?

When I was a professor there was this madness that infected almost all of the students and faculty. It was a pervasive and palpable sense of anxiety and stress, of not having enough time, not having enough resources, of struggling to make it to the finish line. Invariably when I would meet a fellow colleague in the hallway, both of us scampering hastily from one meeting or class to another and I would ask "How are you?" they would reply rapidly in a stressed out fashion, "Oh, you know, it's that time of the semester!"

Now, the funny thing about this response was that they would always say the same thing no matter whether it was the beginning, the middle or the end of the semester! No matter what time of the semester it was, they were stressed out because it was *that time* of the semester!

Now, how is that for living under a spell?

I remember a friend stopping me in the hallway one day. We had just had one of those typical exchanges to which I had replied, "Oh, I'm great, things are going great, thanks for asking."

He paused, held me in his gaze, and then with a quizzical look on his face said, "You always say that you know. Are you really great or are you lying?"

We both laughed and I said, "well even if I wasn't, I would say I was. You know, fake it until you make it." Then looking directly into my friend's eyes with serious intent, I said "you are what you say you are, you know."

And then to break the tension I laughed and said "and I really am great."

As we both walked away laughing, I hoped the lesson took hold for him. It sure did for me. The words we say, whether out loud or silently in our minds cast a spell over our feelings, actions, lives and relationships. They become real in the world.

At some point when we were teenagers Bart made up a funny phrase, a jokey way of saying goodbye to me. And in time I began saying it back to him. He would say "see you later, don't get pregnant." We thought it was funny and silly because we were boys and we couldn't get pregnant.

But what we didn't recognize was the power of language to cast spells and to affect reality. You see the word "not," energetically doesn't exist. It has no effect on the mind or the universe. You cannot attract a "not." If I say "don't think of a pink elephant" you will think of a pink elephant. The "don't" doesn't exist. You have to think of, energetically manifest in positive form what is expressed as a negative, just to understand what was said.

So when Bart and I said to each other "don't get pregnant" the universe heard, and we energetically aligned with or attracted "get pregnant." And that's exactly what happened. Is it any wonder that both of us had our firstborn children in the same way? We both accidentally got our girlfriends pregnant and then married them and had our first child. What else should we have expected to happen when we were issuing the command again and again "Get Pregnant" "Get Pregnant."

Our words cast spells over us when we think and say them and they even cast spells over others. Over other people. Over other objects. Over events. Over everything.

Words have the power of creation.

"In the beginning was the word."

Regardless the religious tradition this is how it all starts: With the word, with the breath, with the beginning of creation.

When children first learn to read and write they feel this magical power in words. They feel the power that words have of making things manifest, of making them real. I remember my youngest son Bodie would make these signs and get such a kick out of them. He would, for example, take some candy and put it on a plate and put a sign next to it saying "These are poison" or more accurately he would write "thes r poisin" and it felt real to him, so very clever and powerful how those words changed things, created a new reality.

I remember sitting with my boys one day talking, out on the trampoline during a rest period in between bouts of furious jumping, play-fighting, flipping and laughing. We lay on the black tramp, the bright sun beaming down upon us and discussed and debated with great earnestness that all-important topic of many boyhood discussions: "If you could have a superpower, what would it be? What is the best superpower?"

At the time Hunter must have been about 12 and Bodie 8. I liked to call them the puppies because they were always crawling on top of each other, wrestling, laughing and pushing each other playfully and lovingly around. Now however, we lay sprawled out, staring up into the big expansive blue sky, focused solely on imagining the experience of and the merits of each different superpower and arguing for our favorites.

"Invisibility would be pretty cool," I said. "You could sneak into places, be an excellent thief and be impossible to catch."

"Yeah that's true, but I think Super Strength would be much better. You could smash anything, defeat anyone. You'd be invincible so you wouldn't have to hide and steal, you could just take anything you wanted." Hunter replied.

"Yeah, but I gotta say, for sure, my absolute favorite would be the power to fly. Oh man, flying would be so awesome!" Of course, I'd been obsessed with flight ever since I was young. "You could soar over the tree tops around our house, fly to school and work and do amazing flying sidekicks." I laughed.

"No guys, that's not it. I've got it. I know what the best super power is." Bodie is often the quiet one. The one who holds back at first, watches and waits and then when he decides to deliver, it is perfectly timed and precisely aimed. "My best super power is the power to create anything."

Silence, as Bodie let the idea sink in.

I watched a small wisp of white cloud move slowly across the azure sky.

"If you want money, you don't have to rob or take it, you just make it. If you want to fly you make a way to fly, a flying surfboard or skateboard and then you fly. And if you want a house, a boat, an island, a whole bunch of food or toys, a swimming pool, a parrot for a pet or a new puppy, you just create it. And if you want any other superpower you make it too."

As Bodie's soft voice washed over me in the sunlight, I felt a lightning bolt of energy shoot through me and could simultaneously hear in my mind Richard Bandler's gravelly voice. He is on stage with a participant from the audience at a Neuro-Hypnotic Repatterning seminar that I am attending, and she is under hypnosis and he is curing her of a severe case of claustrophobia. Her case is so bad that she cannot even ride in a small car or go to the local water parks in Florida where the seminar is held because the water slide tubes are so small. Elevators without mirrors are also very difficult for her to take.

She is sitting upright, eyes closed, in a hypnotic trance and Dr. Bandler is telling her: "In a moment I'm going to snap my fingers and you are going to open your eyes and come out of the trance and then you are going to walk over to that closet at the side of the room here, and go inside, into that dark and tiny space, and we are going to close the door and leave you in there for a while. And yes, you will feel fine and what is more important than how good you will feel is that you will know that if you can do this you can do any fucking thing you want for the rest of your life! And that is a very good feeling!"

After the lightning bolt of energy and the vision shot through my mind, I lay for a few minutes watching the white cloud slowly float by and thought about Bodie's and Bandler's superpower.

"Oh Bro!" Hunter exclaimed. "That's totally right. You're the best Bodilicious! Ultimate creation! The power to make any thing!"

And then at that precise moment, Corey showed up. He landed with a tremendous bounce, like a 500 pound man might bounce, right in the center of the tramp, sending me shooting skyward. And this being some sort of Quantum bounce, the boys remained talking below as the two of us soared up into the blue sky.

"Now you know C, what Bodie is talking about? This is precisely what I've been teaching you. The power I've been giving you. The power to manifest anything you want to be, have or do!"

We reached the peak of our upward arc and dropped back down toward the trampoline far, far below, landing on our backs, the tramp giving in and reality seeming to bend a bit in that familiar dream-like fashion. I noticed that the boys were gone. We had clearly shifted on some level of time-space and I knew that a lesson was about to begin.

"You see C, if everything is energy, then a thought, an intention is energy. If you can let Reiki flow through you, out your hands and into a client's body and energy can be transmitted over long distances, then you can shoot that energy out, out across any distance of time or space in the multi-verse. And to practice this, to play with it, to learn about it, you can get a little more playfully-serious about cloud busting."

"Oh my god, I forgot all about that. Bart and I used to try to cloud bust all the time!"

"Yes C, but you know, we don't try. We do."

The technique that Corey taught me that day for busting clouds involves stretching one hand up toward the sky directly above you and spinning the fingers, while visualizing the energy from the sun and universe spinning down, vortexing into your hand and arm and body. Then you visualize and feel the energy shooting through your chest and out your other arm which is pointed at the cloud of your choice and you see and feel the energy shooting across the sky and into the cloud, exciting and increasing the energy in that cloud of water droplets, making each vibrate faster and mover farther and farther apart until the cloud disappears before your eyes.

My house is perfect for cloud busting. It sits high on a south facing hill, looking over a wide valley toward a forested mountain ridge. The prevailing winds have clouds sweeping across the expansive horizon from side to side, giving you a wide view and lots of targets to play with.

Each time you succeed, each time you see the cloud you have chosen disappear and no others, your power of belief or your ability to believe increases. This is what it means to practice believing. Sometimes we have to make believe first, in order to believe later. And our ability to achieve is directly dependent on our ability to believe. This is what I call The Power of Pretend. Everything I have ever become or been, I have pretended to be first.

Being somewhat scientifically minded, I ran a little experiment one time with myself to test the repeatability of the power. I was visiting my folks in Colorado, at the same house in the mountains that I had been quantum leaping to in order to meet Corey, and I was in charge of the meat on the BBQ grill. It was one of those beautiful sunny days in Colorado with a blue sky, speckled with small white billowy clouds.

Since I had a timer and was flipping the meat every 5 minutes, I decided to try a timed experiment. First I picked out a small cloud and watched it for exactly 5 minutes to make sure it was stable and wasn't disappearing or blowing around in the wind. Then I reset the timer for 5 minutes and began busting the cloud. I repeated the experiment 3 times with 3 different clouds. Each time, I was able to completely disappear the cloud I was aiming at and no others, in less than 3 minutes. Calculate the statistical probability of that happening by random chance if you like, but I can tell you, as they so often say in the sutras "the number is greater than all the sands of the Ganges."

Although it's exhilarating and tons of fun to watch the cloud disappear as you imagined and intended, I have to admit I still haven't found a useful application for the skill of cloud busting, but like ripping a telephone book in half, it is a nice party trick. It is however, a good place to begin practicing and developing your powers of not only telekinesis, but more importantly belief.

As Corey taught me, if you can clear a cloud out of the sky by focusing your energy or your intention on it, then you can clear the clouds of doubt and negativity and limitation out of your own mind. If you can spin energy out of the universe and into physical form, then you can manifest the financial and material abundance in your life that you desire.

"Unfortunately," Corey explained, "while people are more fixated on material reality than they should be, more attached to financial and material abundance than they need to be, they also are full of a number of powerful and limiting beliefs regarding money that keep their true wealth and abundance away from them."

"Beliefs like: It's not possible or likely for me to be wealthy or to make that much money. That's a common one. What else?"

"That it's greedy or stealing, that being wealthy means taking it away from others." I offered.

"Yeah that's the starving hordes argument. There is also the puritanical one that it's superficial or materialistic to want those things, or I don't deserve those things. These are all very common and powerful limiting beliefs."

"Also, it takes a lot of time or luck to get wealthy and that others will get jealous." I added.

"That's a really common one with regard to people's extended families depending on their upbringing. And finally, people are often carrying around some version of, 'wealthy people are greedy or pampered or lazy or stole it and I don't want to be like them.'"

"It's no wonder people can't attract wealth if they are carrying around beliefs like these!" I observed.

"You see what most people don't get C, what they miss is that dollar bills are nothing more than symbols. They are symbolic representations, anchors, encapsulations of someone else's time, someone else's sacred life force and purpose, someone else's spiritual energy. Thus, in one sense they are sacred spiritual energy. Not materialistic. Not evil. But in fact good, part of a sacred spiritual exchange of value and time and life force energy."

"And if what you are doing in the world is good C, if what you are giving to others is of value than the simplest measure of the good you are doing in the world is how much money you are making."

"It's all energy."

"Dollar bills are just energy encapsulated in a material form. They are the energy of creation. Wealth is a creative force not a thing. You need it to have your superpower. Wealth gives you your rightful superpower of creation."

"But unfortunately most of you don't see it that way. Most are filled instead with limiting beliefs about wealth that push it away from you."

"You think there is a finite amount of it. You think it is a pie split between people and that some will get more and some not enough. You think that if wealth flows to you then it can't flow through you. You think that there is a limited amount of energy in the universe. You think the infinite and ever-expanding multi-verse is limited."

"You think that dollar bills are material manifestations, less than energy, not sacred, but profane. You think that material wealth prevents you from connecting to the spiritual plane. You think that spiritual energy cannot be translated into material form. You think that dollar bills cannot represent and symbolize the sacred spiritual energy and effort and time of another human being and thus they cannot be sacred."

"You think your body is not a spirit."

"You think your thoughts are not real."

"You think energy is not matter."

"You are wrong."

"Your thinking is your problem."

"Actually it's your lack of thinking that's the problem."

"All these things I've been listing are not examples of thinking. They are examples of beliefs and those beliefs are based on remembering falsehoods that others said to you. So you see, the problem is that you have been remembering what others believe instead of thinking and believing for yourself."

"These remembered beliefs are the only things holding you back from happiness, preventing you from doing the impossible and stopping you from living the life of your dreams."

"The Mind is the Battle ground," I remember Corey powerfully saying. "This is the only place you need to fight. This is where you need to put forth your most heroic efforts."

Corey taught me that if you can change your thinking (which you can) you will change your feelings.

If your feelings change (which they are going to) then your behavior will change.

If your behavior changes (which it will) then the results you get from the world will change.

And if the results you get change (which they are right now) then you will feel better.

It happens first internally in the mind, then externally in the world. And when it does happen you will shout with joy "Holy Shift! Shift Happens!"

There are more people with troubles in their minds than in their finances. There are more people with difficulties in their minds than with their physical health. There are more people with problems in their minds than problems in their relationships. There are more people with a lack of financial or any kind of abundance in their minds than in their lives. There are more people fighting and dying in their minds than on all the battle fields of the world put together.

And those who are suffering in their minds are suffering in their lives.

And let me tell you this: Those who have won in their lives, won first in their minds long ago. Because they won in their minds first they are the ones living the life of their dreams now.

So before anything, you have got to win the battle in your mind.

Before you try to control your external reality, before you try to change the way your partner behaves or the way people treat you, you have to control the way you think, the energy you emit so you can get back the energy you want to attract.

You have to learn to control your thoughts, so you can control your feelings, so you can control your actions, so you can get the results you want.

This type of control is important because we are manifesting all the time. And if you don't control your thoughts and emotions, if you don't control your energetic focus and actions, you will manifest your worst nightmares instead of your greatest dreams.

Corey reminded me of this with a powerful leap that landed us on a dark city street, late at night. I looked around at the towering skyscrapers, felt the humid night air and knew we were in Atlanta. It was after 2:00 am and within the hour I would be getting arrested, handcuffed, thrown in the back of a paddy wagon and taken to Fulton County Jail for the worst jail experience of my life.

"Dude, I know where we are Corey. This is not good," I said.

"Relax C. Nothing is going to happen to us. It already happened anyway, we are just going to get to watch it happen to your past self." Corey was laughing, apparently taking great pleasure in my fear.

Years before, in the time we had now traveled to, I was in Atlanta to corner coach my friend and old-time training partner, Mark Selbee, in his first Heavy Weight World Title Kickboxing defense, and after his win we celebrated long into the night. Apparently I didn't drink as much as everyone else because when they all passed out, I was still awake and decided to walk around the city a bit to clear my head.

"That was an intense experience for me Corey, or us, or whatever. You know that. I was arrested, spent the entire night and next day in jail. I had no idea if I'd be able to get bailed out and almost missed my flight back home. And man, Fulton County was nothing like the times I went to jail in Kansas. It was downright scary as shit. Seriously man!"

"Yeah that's right C, I remember. Now let me ask you, do you remember what happened before you got arrested?"

"You mean before I got caught trespassing in the subway tunnels?" The charges, funnily enough, would eventually include, in addition to criminal trespass, two terrorist charges under the Patriot Act: all for walking down a subway tunnel. "I don't know, I was just walking around looking at the city, I gave that homeless dude 20 bucks, not much really."

"Let me rephrase the question C. What happened in your thoughts? What were you thinking before you got arrested?"

"Oh yeah, I remember. Of course! I was walking around the city all hyped up from the fight and the after-fight party and was very intense, felt tons of energy coursing through me and I remember thinking 'I want to see something real. Show me something real.'"

"And you got something real alright."

"No shit! I wanted to see the real city, the real side of life, the gritty, tough base of it all. And Holy Shit, that's exactly what I got, huh?"

"Instant Manifestation C."

"It happens quite often with what I call Power Peaks. When you are extremely emotional, energetic or feeling powerful emotions about something, you can quite often experience instant manifestation. In this case you instantly manifested a negative experience."

"Well, actually it wasn't; there is no such thing as a negative experience. It was a frightening and fucked up experience but it makes a great story and you enjoy it now, so all in all it was a good experience, but at the time I'm sure it felt like a negative one, so we will call it that." Corey said as an aside, never passing up an opportunity to reinsert an important lesson.

"So you instantly manifested a negative experience because you were power peaking emotionally and energetically from the fight and the night."

"Most often people power peak and instantly manifest negative experiences out of fear. This is extremely important to understand because fear is a powerful emotion and it can attract exactly what you don't want and push away what you want."

"That's true Corey, that's why we say in combat 'Fear causes hesitation and hesitation causes your worst fears to come true.'"

"Yes, Fear is a powerful attractor and repulsor, all emotions are, whether they are positive or negative. So you have to be careful C, about what you put your attention on especially when giving it a lot of emotional energy. Put your mind on what you want, not on what you don't want. Focus on your desire, on the good not the bad." And then he was gone and the leap was over.

There are probably a fair number of you who are reading this who think I'm crazy. Who think these things are made up, that they are not real, that this is all bullshit.

And you know I could be wrong about all of this.

Or not.

For many people, especially many rationally minded people it is difficult to accept much of what I claim here.

Is quantum leaping for real?

Is there another world after death?

Is God for real?

Is belief or faith in anything that there doesn't seem to be physical evidence of just self-delusion?

There are many who question the belief in anything that can't be measured, quantified, physically sampled or observed.

Cynics and skeptics and materialists will often argue that these forms of energetic manifestation are mere coincidence. Whether it's cloud busting or manifesting, it is simply coincidence, correlation not causation.

Those addicted to the present material reality and who can only see its physical form will claim that I'm adding an interpretation that is not supported by the physical facts and that is not needed to causally explain the physical facts. They will argue that there is no way to measure or quantify or verify or prove the existence, nor the causal connection, between my thoughts or intentions, and physical reality.

Of course I do have the many physical changes in my life, wealth, success and happiness as evidence, but they might call these coincidences.

When you meet these kind of limited views, these addictions to the physical, material and present reality, whether in yourself or others, especially in yourself, be kind but ask yourself or others this simple question:

Is love real?

Have you experienced it before?

Have you experienced its loss or its absence?

Think about someone you love, someone close to you, picture them in your mind, their hair, their face, hear their voice and that special thing they often do.

Now think of someone you have loved and lost. Think about how you felt without them, the sadness, the anger, the loneliness.

Are these emotional experiences you are having real? Yes of course they are. But they are impossible to prove. They can't be measured, photographed or quantified. Love cannot be proven to exist anymore than God can. But we know it exists because we experience it. We feel it. We see what it does to us and others. We can see and measure its effect on the world.

So we know that love is real because we experience it and we experience its effects.

It causes you to act in certain very specific ways. We all know, even psychologists know, that love or any emotion has a causal effect on our behavior. And yet we have never discovered a way to measure love or any other emotion.

The same is true of these quantum leaps, these energy exercises, these magical mantras: We know, I know that they are real because I experience them. Every day I experience them in my life and feel their effects just as assuredly as I know love when I feel it.

Now my scientific friends might actually argue with me on one point and that being that in reality love can be measured. When we feel the emotion of love, it is related to a chemical reaction in the body and brain and the presence of oxytocin. When different areas of the brain are active it can be recorded and thus in many ways when we are feeling love or some other emotion there is a sort of physical evidence of it.

Others might say this makes love Un-real, an illusion. Our mind is tricked by serotonin and oxytocin to feel and think a certain way, that it's no more real than an acid trip. It's simply a chemical reaction in the brain.

This one I find very interesting because love is even less "real" than that. A chemical reaction is really just an energetic reaction. All things, of course, at the sub-atomic level are just bundles of energy, waves of energy moving back and forth, in and out of existence.

So when we feel love it is really an energetic experience.

Just like everything we experience is.

If I jump spin heel kick you, dear reader, in the head for example, energy will transfer from my heel to your head. A lot of energy. So much energy, in fact, that your neck would break and you would most likely be dead before you hit the ground. Now, your death would be real. It would be very real to you and your family. And it was energy that caused it.

Now, you might argue it wasn't "energy," it was the material physicality of my foot that did the damage. However, it is much more accurate to describe the damage as being caused by energy. In fact impact is measured as force and in physics the equation to measure force is F = M x A or Force Equals Mass Times Acceleration. The mass of the foot and the body-weight behind it, multiplied by the speed at which it is traveling yield, or create the force or the energy of the impact. It is the absorption of this energy that causes the damage to physical structures and thus causes death.

"Remember C, how we discussed earlier that every thing in the universe is energy. How there are only four known forces in the universe?" His voice echoed in my head.

"Yes," I replied. "The strong and weak nuclear forces, gravity and electro-magnetism."

"Excellent C. Now I'm going to go out on a limb here and say that these can be broken down further and that soon we will re-define classical physics and recognize that there are only two physical forces in the universe."

"The strong and weak nuclear forces—forces inside the atom—can be understood as demonstrations of the same force: The Attractive Force. And gravity also, on a much larger scale is an example of The Attractive Force. It is demonstrated on a microcosmic level as the strong and weak force in the atom and on the macrocosmic level as gravity between planets and objects."

"Electro-magnetism, or Electricity and Magnetism are often thought of as separate forces because they are often seen to be working alone. However it is more accurate to see them as a single Electro-Magnetic Force. Electricity requires both a positive and a negative pole in order to work in the same way that magnetism requires or creates polarity. And because of this polarity, electro-magnetism can switch between attraction and repulsion. So electromagnetism in any form is an example of The Force of Attraction and The Force of Repulsion."

"So we have only two forces in the universe: The gravitational or sub-atomic force of Attraction and the electro-magnetic force of Attraction or Repulsion. So at its most elemental, Everything in the multi-verse is either an energy of Attraction or Repulsion. That's it, there is nothing else."

"In other words C, to simplify it all as much as much as possible: There are only two forces in the universe:"

"Attraction and Repulsion."

"Push and Pull. Toward and Away."

"Love and Fear."

"That's it, nothing else."

"Yin and Yang. Black and White. Positive and Negative Poles."

"Now, if we want to attract anything in our life, an experience or thing or person, we have to align with it energetically, with its presence not its absence. This is crucial to understand because many people are actually pushing away the things they want by focusing on the lack of those things in their lives. It's much like the drowning person who keeps pushing away the life saver they are reaching for. With each splash and attempt to grasp it, they make waves which push it farther and farther away. Come with me C," Corey said and then we leaped.

I found myself standing next to Corey at the top of a cliff, in Alaska overlooking a waterfall and a deep, dark blue pool of cold water. The lush boreal rainforest surrounding us was filled with sitka spruce, western hemlock and yellow cedar, while the ground beneath these swaying giants was covered in mosses and ferns. I recognized this place from my early twenties.

Almost twenty years earlier Tim and I stood on this exact spot, naked, shivering and laughing, as we tried to conjure up the courage to jump. The cliff of dark polished stone rose probably about 60 feet above the water, while a torrent of cold, white cascading falls leapt off its edge and out into space. Tim and I swam in the pool first, on that day so many years ago, diving down under the water, checking to see if it was deep enough for a jump. Then we climbed and hiked, naked through the forest, like primordial cavemen, to the top of the falls for our jump.

I can still remember being at Tim's house after his funeral and going through his old photo albums with family and friends. Tim's mom found a picture of us both, bare ass naked below the falls, dancing and laughing in the cascading water, but couldn't tell exactly who it was. I admitted the two naked culprits were Tim and I and we all had a good laugh remembering old times.

This time, I once again stood above the falls with a dear friend and knew we were about to jump. As I looked over at Corey though, something caught my eye. There was a tattoo on his right shoulder that I do not have. At that particular point in my life, I had only one tattoo: a birthday gift I gave myself for my fortieth birthday of the Korean Hangul characters for Tae Kwon Do, right above my heart.

Seeing this new tattoo on Corey and knowing I was going to get it at some point in my future intrigued me, as did the tattoo's design and meaning. It was round, two words in the shape of a yin yang symbol, with one word—Intend—in black letters, and the other word—Allow—outlined not filled in, so together they gave the same contrasting, black and white effect as the traditional symbol itself.

"Intend and Allow, huh? Tell me about your tattoo Corey. *Law of Attraction* stuff, like in *The Secret,* right?"

"Yes C, that is correct and that is why we are here today, standing on the brink of a death defying precipice." He laughed and motioned toward the cliff before us. I know you have already been working with some of this stuff, but we are going to take it to a deeper level. I want you to really know, understand and experience the Law of Attraction because in all honesty, if there was one core principle underlying everything I'm teaching you, one single foundation upon which all MindBody Mastery rests, it is this Law, the Law that explains how all things, people and events energetically attract each other and manifest each other into their own experience."

"So you remember how we were just discussing that every 'thing' in the universe is actually energy, waves vibrating at specific frequencies?"

"Yes I do, no matter, no particles, just energy, only waves. Every form of physical manifestation is simply crystalized energy."

"Good C, that's it, now what is important to realize about this is that if you want any 'thing' in your life, if you want any material manifestation you must first get into alignment with its energetic frequency. You can think of this as being like radio frequencies: if you want to hear a certain station you have to tune into that frequency. So, if you want a specific 'thing' or 'event' to manifest in your life, before you pay attention to the physical, to the material manifestation of it and the physical acts needed to get it, you must first get into energetic alignment with it. Many times people are pushing away the very thing they say they want because instead of aligning with it energetically, they align with or focus on their lack of it."

"This all sounds very familiar Corey. You sound exactly like Esther and Jerry Hicks, in their great book *The Law of Attraction* or in any of their wonderful lecture series about *Getting Into the Vortex*."

"Yes C, that's exactly it. Abraham's teachings, as brought to us by Esther and Jerry are my favorite, most powerful, most concise and precise articulations of the Law of Attraction that I have ever come across. And that *Universal Law—The Law of Attraction*—sates that like attracts like that two things on the same vibrational frequency will attract each other over space and time."

"And if you think back to our earlier conversations on nonlocality, entanglement and resonant frequency you can begin to see how changing the vibration of your thoughts will do much more than change how you feel and behave. It will actually change the external world around you and through the cascading ripple effect of reality, everyone and everything in it."

"We've already discussed how you can energetically and emotionally change the physiological structure of your brain and body, but now we are going to go way beyond that. We are going to step outside of our own selves and talk about how we can energetically change the physical form of the universe that surrounds us."

"You are going to learn to literally change the world with your own thoughts."

"That sounds great Corey, but of course my first and last question is How?"

"That C, is not the question to ask. It's our focus on the How that prevents us from getting what we want. First and most importantly focus on the Why."

"Why do you want that thing, person or experience? Why will it make your life better? As you align with the Why, as you focus your desire in greater and greater strength, the How will be revealed to you, just like the road is revealed to you at night, one stretch at a time by your headlights."

"In much the same way C, as with many things we have discussed about the nature of reality most people have it all backward. Because people are so focused on physical reality they think that if there is anything they want, they must work for it, they must focus on how to get it done. They believe that they must take physical action and must use their body to get what they want in life. They say for example, 'I want something, so I'm going to go work for it, get a job or do whatever, use my body, start working toward that goal.'"

"But they also believe that it might not be possible to get what they want that they might not be successful. And they are afraid of feeling disappointed so they say, 'I'm not going to really dwell on it too much though, focus on it, or want or desire it too much, because then if I don't get it I will feel terrible.'"

"They attempt to attract their desire physically but they push it way mentally, emotionally, energetically."

"A common example of this will illustrate the point. Many people will say, 'I really want a life-long loving partner, but that seems like too much to want and if I don't get it, I'll feel disappointed. So I won't think about it or focus on it with my mind or heart, instead I'll just go out and date, I'll act on it with my body.'"

"But then of course they don't get what they really want because they aren't focused on what they really want. They're focused on dating instead of being focused on finding that one person who may be their life mate and partner."

"Okay, yeah Corey, I see that kind of thing all the time. People going through the motions physically, but not mentally, separating the mind and body."

"Good C, instead use the mind to focus on what you want, think about it, dream about it, get in alignment with it, appreciate its qualities, intend to have it with your mind, act with your mind and attach with your mind to your goal first. This will put you into energetic alignment with your goal. This will help you tune into its operational frequency."

"And then, allow with our body. Don't act right away, don't worry about it. Let it come to you. Have faith and allow it to be. When the right action arises by itself you will know and your body will follow, it will flow and it will feel almost effortless. You still have to act, but your actions will flow. They will be unforced, powerful and in alignment with the object of your desire."

"I developed two mantras that I say every morning which help focus me on both aspects of Intending and Allowing."

"The first, I taught you earlier: The 'Who is the Master?' mantra."

"Since you are the type of person who by nature has done more Intending than Allowing in life (and are a bit of a control freak some might say, or a Type A personality according to others, or a 'real go getter,' a busy beaver, someone who just can't sit still) that first mantra fits the intending side of you perfectly. I have taught it to many others and they have all used it to great effect. It reminds us that we are masters of our own selves and our own creation, that we are 100% responsible for it all and it allows flexibility so we can focus the intention on whatever we want to that day or week or month or moment."

"The second mantra however, develops the Allowing side of us. A side that for you C is a bit underdeveloped."

Corey was right, I have to admit. I've always been a bit of a control freak.

Once, in fifth grade we were assigned to do history projects in groups of four and I asked the teacher if I could do the entire project by myself, even though that would be more work. He asked me why and finally I admitted, "Well, if I'm in a group nobody will do things right, they'll just screw it up and the project won't be as good as I can do alone or it'll be even more work to fix their screw ups then to just do it myself." Fortunately, he explained to me that learning to work with others was more important than the project itself and then promptly put me in a group.

So it was a nice change of pace that this mantra just came to me that it wasn't something I tried to create or make up. This of course is fitting because it is about allowing after all. It's not a mantra that one intends to create. It is a mantra that one allows to come to them.

So here is the story of how it came to me:

I had signed up to take my first flying lesson. It was a longtime dream of mine ever since reading *Illusions* by Richard Bach. Finally I would be in a small plane, flying it, controlling its flight, looking down on the tree tops and city, I was so excited.

But, I needed my passport to fly and for the life of me I couldn't find it. I looked everywhere at home; it wasn't with my boy's passports or anywhere else I could imagine it would be. Finally, knowing I could also use my birth certificate which I had, I gave up looking for the passport. I had a strong feeling of confidence that I would eventually find it and if not, I could always get a new one. And since I didn't need it right away, I decided that it would come to me, that in time it would just pop up. I wasn't even aware at the moment, but I had just performed a powerful act of Allowing.

Then about a week later, the day before my first flight, I was in my office at Humboldt State University, working on a chapter for a book about environmental writing and I grabbed a familiar book off the shelf and out of its pages dropped my passport, landing with a cosmic, earth-shattering thud, at my feet. On pure inspiration, as if the words were being breathed out of me, I turned toward the window, held my hands open wide and low, arms spread out and said, four times:

I am open, Oh Universe

To everything you bring me

And grateful for its time and manner in coming.

This mantra also allows for some slight changes. At times I will replace "Oh Universe" with "Oh Great Creator" or "My Dear Vortex" or "God" or "Universal Energies" or depending on where you are geographically "Rolling Prairie," "Great Desert," "Grand forest," "Lush Valley," "Big City."

You can use any specific language that speaks powerfully to you.

Taken together these two mantras encompass for me the entire scope, depth and energetic vibration of both Intending and Allowing.

This mantra is especially powerful and helpful, especially reassuring and liberating when you are feeling out of control. Saying it repeatedly when you are feeling like the world is shoving you around will bring a warm blanket of comfort, hope and promise around you as you let yourself melt further into the loving arms of your future.

The simple truth is that we don't Receive what we don't Believe.

We must Believe it to Receive it. We must Believe it to Achieve it.

"So, are you ready to experience this process of Intending and Allowing again C?" Corey asked.

"You bet Corey, lay it on me."

"Okay C, it's time to go and in order to get there, we are going to jump. At the same time as me, I want you to say out loud 'I intend to jump off this cliff and land safely in the water.' Then, we will jump, and then you must allow, you must let go and trust your intention. If you do you won't feel fear, but if you don't you will be scared."

"Oh yeah, I know exactly what you mean. This is why I can't handle rollercoasters, I can't let go, so I'm scared. I don't allow."

"Yes C, that's always been a cute weakness of yours." Corey replied laughing. "Now let's experience how to get over it. Get ready to Intend and Allow"

He counted to three and we both shouted out our intention and jumped together. My feet lifted off the cold wet stone and I was sailing out into the empty air and then falling, faster than the water beside me, dropping down like a rock to disappear in the water with a splash.

The entire way down, I felt only the exhilaration of letting go.

Once you start working with this process you will have the experience I had, where almost everything I intended I got.

I was intending open parking spaces where there usually were none and getting them.

I set an intention to move to a new house: I wanted a view of both the sunrise and the sunset, I wanted a place like my parent's home, a fire place, a long scenic view, more sun than was possible in our pacific northwest climate, a small town feel that was close to my Tae Kwon Do academy and I got it, found it, exactly it. It was the very first house the boys and I looked at in fact.

I intended to fall in love, in order to feel my heart move again and it did.

I intended to earn $5,000.00 more per month and I got it.

I set an intention for which publisher would publish our anthologies *The Pacific Crest Trailside Reader* and I got exactly the publisher I chose.

I set an intention to make more money in my first year of coaching than I made in my previous year as a tenure track professor and I did it.

The list goes on and on and on.

However, every now and then you don't get what you intend, you don't get what you want.

What you will discover, like I did, is that most of the time you get what you intend, you get what you want. And the few times you don't get what you want, you get what you need. Which is of course even better.

That's why when I do intending work, when I program what I want to manifest, after I say and visualize and feel clearly what I want to attract and manifest, I say and feel "This or something better!"

So you can walk through life with total faith that you will always get whatever you want and the few times you don't get what you want, you will get exactly what you need.

During this same period when he was teaching me about Intending and Allowing, Corey focused on the subject of financial abundance.

First, he deeply ingrained in me through all of the stories and experiences in this chapter the crystal clear realization that we are either attracting or repulsing that which we desire and we are doing it with our thoughts, our beliefs, our language, our feelings and finally with our actions or lack of them. He taught me to energetically align with financial abundance and to make believe until we believe and to use the following techniques to attract the avalanches of abundant wealth we desire and deserve.

In order to clear any limiting or negative beliefs that are pushing your wealth away from you, take some time to reflect, to go inside and to journal about how you think and feel about wealth. Were there things you heard growing up from your parents or others about limitations around money. If you were giving a sermon on the evils of money what would you say? "You are greedy and superficial and evil to want it. There is only so much to go around. The rich take from others. It's impure, not spiritual, lazy, unethical, impossible, not likely, etc."

Write all that stuff down. Then write the opposite of each limiting belief and negative feeling. "There is an infinite amount of material abundance and wealth. The more that flows to me, the more I can flow through me and give away. When I charge full value for my services I empower others to earn more and increase their potential; this is not taking, it is giving."

Now create a mantra, an affirmation about financial wealth and repeat it 10 times every day with energy and emotion. Cast this spell on yourself and your world each and every day: "There is an infinite amount of wealth in the universe and it flows to me and through me in avalanches of abundance because I deserve it and I can and will earn it. Each dollar I earn is a measure of the good I am providing the world. The more money I make the more people I help. I have an infinite number of ways of earning and attracting financial abundance and freedom."

Next journal about and reflect on what greater financial abundance really means to you. We don't really want a stack of cash. We want what that stack of cash can give us. What is it that you want? College tuition for your children? To travel the world? To quit your job? To buy a house or a car? To be able to pay a loved one's hospital bills? Write about and feel about what that wealth will mean for you. This is called fueling up your emotional gas tank. This is about psyching yourself up before the battle, about getting in the zone before the game. This is about creating enough emotion to put you into motion.

Create an image that represents what your new wealth will mean to you: a collage of images and words and numbers and dollar signs that represents your newfound wealth. And create a check from the Universe to you and write out a specific amount on it, the amount you want to manifest in total or per month or whatever. Be specific and be clear.

Each day, look at your check and image of wealth, repeat your affirmation and visualize in meditation what you will do with your wealth. See and feel all the things you can and will do with your new-found wealth that align with your deepest values and desires. Go ahead and watch yourself do it all: put your child through college and medical school, take that vacation to Greece and help the neediest in your community. Enjoy the feelings of doing these wonderful things and attach those powerful feelings toward generating more financial abundance.

Now it's time to take action. We call this "Getting into the State and Then…" In order to be effective, in order to find our flow, in order to attract and energetically align with our goal we always want to get into the right emotional and energetic state and Then begin working on it. If you work on your project while being stressed about it, fearful, frustrated or in any other negative state, you will be pushing your goal away energetically, even as you struggle and strive physically. Just like the drowning man reaching for the life saver that continually bobs out of reach pushed there by his struggling.

Instead, before we reach for our goal, we want to be energetically aligned with it, attracted to it, and these techniques will do that for you.

After having spent some time aligning and energizing yourself, begin brainstorming those ideas you already have and be open to new ones coming in. Where is your earning potential outside of your salary? What is it that you like to do? What are you good at? What is that one curiously weird idea you've always had? How can you earn more money, get more customers, etc.?

Return to this list daily, add to it and continue to add to it, until one or several clear ideas emerge. Then with each of these, answer such questions as: What would it look and feel like to earn money doing this? Where am I now in relation to this goal? What are some of the steps along the way? What things will I need to get and do in order to put this into action? Where can I find a model or a mentor who has done this before? This will get you started.

Then get a partner or more than one person to join you in a weekly Master Mind Group where you discuss what you are doing in your own lives to manifest greater health and wealth. Help each other brainstorm and come up with ideas. Hold each other accountable to take actions and celebrate each other's successes. Use this group not only to strategize but also to motivate yourself and each other. This suggestion comes from Napoleon Hill's classic book *Think and Grow Rich*. He dramatically emphasizes that if he had only one piece of advice to give someone on how to get rich, it would be to start a Master Mind Group and keep one going until you die.

Or get a Professional Coach, someone who specializes in transformational change and attracting wealth. After all, this is what Coaches like I do on a daily basis: We show people how make their dreams come true.

And once you have this long list of all these different steps and tasks and things to do, make sure that each day you take one step toward your goal. Each day, do one thing to work on that new project, that business idea, that new venture that is going to bring it all in, tumbling down around you in avalanches of abundant health and wealth.

Some days you will work more than others. Maybe Sunday you will take off. But each day take at least one small step toward your goal and on the days when you are inspired take great big running leaps and bounds, until you find yourself flowing along amidst the cascade of abundant health and wealth that has become your every day life experience.

I wonder what new ideas you will have, dear reader, after reading, this about ways to attract abundant wealth to you and what immense value you can give to others and the world in order to boomerang back that energy in the form of great big stacks of cash and checks and riches.

And I'm curious what you will do with your newfound financial abundance, what pleasures and experiences you will have, who you will help and what doors of opportunity will open to you, as you find that one dollar leads to others and more lead to even more, as one idea builds on another and you find yourself carried away in an avalanche of abundant and creative ideas and opportunities for earning as both your bank accounts and life purpose become so fulfilled that they are overflowing with rich rewards that cascade off of you and onto everyone around you limitlessly and forever.

I wonder.

Don't you wonder too?

CHAPTER NINE

THE END IS THE BEGINNING

> *"Our deepest fear is not that we are inadequate. Our deepest fear is that we are powerful beyond measure. It is our light, not our darkness that most frightens us."*
>
> —Marianne Williamson

On this particular leap, it felt like Corey and I were a mere presence, not really there at all or maybe like we were watching it unfold on a movie screen.

I saw myself driving on a wonderfully scenic road, on bluffs overlooking the ocean near my home. GrandMaster and Mrs. Yi were in the truck with me and we were looking out across massive rocky sea stacks toward a slowly undulating pacific and a sky filled with the brightest hues of red, orange and purple you could ever imagine.

I remembered the moment very clearly. It was one of the first times that I had ever teased my Korean Tae Kwon Do instructor when he was being serious. I had been with Grandmaster for over 30 years, since I was 11, and in that time he had become a father to me, but still the respect I had for him and his serious demeanor often meant I adopted a reserved and serious manner around him.

"Wow, what a beautiful sunset!" Mrs. Yi exclaimed. "I just love the sunset. Look at those colors. It is sooo beautiful!"

The colors washed out of the sky and bled down onto the deep blue sea below. Beams of bright light shot straight out at us, refracting off thin clouds and spraying ocean waves. It seemed as if both the sky above and the ocean below were on fire.

"Yes, but you shouldn't like sunsets too much." GrandMaster began, in his usual slow and serious tone. Although a very kind man with a quick and funny wit, GrandMaster was also a serious and quiet man. A soldier and survivor, a veteran of countless battles who had lost many friends and loved ones along the way, he also knew much about the hard and painful sides of life.

"You know when a soldier sees the sunset, he thinks of those he has lost, the ones who died and sunsets often make soldiers sad. You should like the sunrise more. Don't like the sunset too much. The sunrise is much better." GrandMaster finished in a serious and knowing way.

I heard the wisdom and compassion in his words and the memories of loss, and still I had to say something. "Oh sir!" I exclaimed, laughing. "You are way too serious!"

I could hear Mrs. Yi's giggling erupt in the backseat and wash over me as I continued, stealing a furtive glance to the side at GrandMaster to see if he was offended. His face was a comical mask of mock surprise and a beaming smile.

"Sunsets are just as good as sunrises, sir. You should like both!"

Mrs. Yi was laughing in the backseat hysterically, while we both chuckled in the front and I sat amazed at myself for "correcting" my GrandMaster on something.

"You know C." Corey said. We all love beginnings and lament endings. We love births and lament deaths. We celebrate marriages and are disappointed by divorces."

"Yes that's true, when I first got divorced I definitely lamented it as a loss and saw it as an ending, as the ending of my family and marriage and love and much of my life."

"Right C. You definitely did not and could not at the time, see it for the beginning that it was, the beginning that it is."

"Yes that's true, but now Corey, today I see the divorce and that difficult time as the beginning of a new life for me, a life of deeper and more fulfilling purpose, of greater joy and self-direction, the beginning of the wonderful life I am leading today."

"Right C, now and then you are getting it."

"This brings us to the last Universal Law we will discuss. You could call it *The Law of Cycles and Circles,* or *The Law of Endings and Beginnings.* Just as there is no beginning or ending on a circle, this law states: 'Every ending is a beginning, and every beginning is an ending.'"

"Every birth is the End of that spirit's time in the blissful soul realm and every death is the Beginning of that person's next spirit journey back into bliss. Every marriage is the End of two single lives and every divorce is the Beginning of two separate lives."

"In fact when we wrap our head around the idea from Quantum Physics that in the multi-verse of space-time there are many times occurring at once, the entire notion of endings and beginnings begins to dissolve. In cyclical or ever-present time, where does the circle begin and where does it end?"

"Of course, this is really just a different way of expressing the first Universal Law, The *Law of Change,* which brings us here in the end, all the way back to the beginning."

There was a swoosh and a pop and in an instant the scene on the ocean cliff-side and the laughter dissolved and Corey and I materialized in the corner of a partially darkened and quiet room. I saw a group of students sitting on the floor, cross legged, holding thermometers in their hands. I could make out my small 11-year-old form and I watched my younger self attentively listen to the instructor.

Corey had taken me back to when I first learned Biofeedback at the world famous Meninger's Institute in Topeka, Kansas. I was lucky enough to participate in a rare program there, where we were shown films and demonstrations of miraculous feats of mind over body healing and mastery and then we were taught the beginning methods ourselves.

At that time Meninger's was especially famous for one of its youngest patients, a boy who had been diagnosed with an inoperable brain tumor. The cancerous tumor was so large that it couldn't be cut away and since it was in his brain, radiation couldn't be used nor could chemotherapy.

The boy loved playing the video arcade game Asteroids, not one many people are familiar with now, but it was popular at the time. In the game, you flew your space ship around and shot asteroids out of the sky. So in his biofeedback work the boy would visualize shooting and blowing up that tumor in his head. All day long, literally for hours every day, he would get to Alpha state and shoot that tumor. Eventually when tested again, he had shrunk the tumor from the size of a baseball to the size of a pea and it had become benign.

As we noted earlier, the MindBody, your neurophysiology doesn't know the difference between what is experienced, remembered or imagined. So by using visualizations and other conscious techniques, we can affect and control physiological processes that are normally unconscious, like the flow of blood, white blood cells, immune response and the experience of pain. As with any of our other visualizations, if we get into a meditative state and visualize ourselves doing and succeeding at what we want, then our body will more naturally and readily do that. So whether it's visualizing faster and more complete healing or pain leaving our body, if we do it first with our mind, then our body will follow.

"What are we doing here?" I whispered to Corey. Although no one in the room could hear us because we weren't on the exact same quantum plane as they were, I still found myself wanting to whisper so as not to disrupt the quiet class.

We were at that moment, I recalled, learning how to control blood flow by raising and lowering the temperature of our hands. First we were taught to increase the blood flow to both hands, watching as the thermometers recorded higher temperatures. Then we decreased the blood flow and brought the temperature back down. Then they had us raising the temperature of one hand and lowering that of the other and then switching. I remember thinking how amazing it was that I could learn to do it so quickly and easily and I began wondering how many other things you could do with biofeedback.

"I wanted you to see this C, because I wanted you to know something really important." He paused, waited until we made eye contact and then held my gaze firmly. "You have been doing this a long time. The stuff I'm teaching you isn't new, it's ancient wisdom and it's not new to you either. You have been learning and doing this stuff your entire life C. This has always been your path."

"That's true, isn't it?" I realized. The free video I created on my www.MindBodyMasteryCoaching.com website for example that teaches people how to cure headaches, uses the exact biofeedback techniques I was taught when I was 11 and acupressure points that I learned from Grandmaster Yi when I was in my teens and twenties and Neuro-Linguistic Programming that I learned in my 30's and 40's.

The "headache cure" I developed can actually be used to decrease or get rid of pain from any area of the body, even without using the acupressure points.

First you get into your meditative state, at Alpha. Then you visualize the pain in your body as being either a bright red color or a dark, ugly brownish-black color. Imagine a hole opening in your body, like at the top of your head or end of your toe and visualize the color flowing out of this hole. Watch as it leaves your body and turns into little bubbles that float away on the breeze and pop in the sunlight. Continue with this visualization until all the painful color is gone.

Then visualize a cool blue color or a warm golden glowing color, replacing the painful color and filling in all the spaces that are left, filling you up completely.

179

While you are doing this visualization have someone ask you repeatedly these three questions: "Where is your pain?" "What color is your pain?" "What shape is your pain?" You will not answer the questions at all, you will just keep visualizing as they ask them again and again.

After a couple minutes, they can re-phrase the questions and put them in past tense, so they become, "Where was your pain?" "What color was your pain?" "What shape was your pain?"

And they will continue to ask these questions for a few more minutes, until your pain is gone.

"And in addition to the biofeedback C, you can use your gratitudes and powerful positive questions to speed healing. As you will recall, white blood cells, those most associated to healing are the most responsive to emotion. So you have got to link your questions and gratitudes to the feelings, the emotions of feeling good, healing and being healthy and vital."

"So thank your body for a fast and complete recovery and feel really good about it, *before* it has happened. And repeatedly ask yourself questions like: "What is the quickest and most complete healing I can imagine? How will I feel when I'm totally healed? How wonderful does it feel to be free from pain and to feel good, healthy and vital?"

"You can use all of these methods to heal the body C, and you can even use them to leave the body!"

"Yeah, I know," I interjected excitedly. "I remember when I had my first outer body experience ever. It was when I was studying with Shadowhawk."

"That's right C. And you know these quantum leaps we are taking? They aren't any different from what Shadowhawk was teaching you in your late teens and early twenties. In precisely the same way that he used drums, rattles, chanting and guided meditation to take you to Alpha and beyond, you are learning through hypnosis and Neuro Linguistic Programming and meditation to do the same thing, for yourself and others. I want you to see that you really have been doing this for a long time."

He passed his hand in front of my eyes, just a slow swipe down in front of them and they closed for just a second. When I opened them we were outside.

I recognized where we were immediately: in the dark next to a steaming sweat lodge where Shadowhawk first taught me about dreamtime and about journeying out of the body. Shadowhawk was a Lakota medicine man who, thanks to an introduction from my mentor and friend Lavetta, took me under his wing and began to teach me the fundamental principles and practices of Lakota spirituality, medicine and meditation.

I still recall in vivid and minute detail my first outer body experience and the tactile sensation of re-entering my physical body. I was 16 at the time and the experience forever altered and expanded my consciousness. Although I have had many outer body experiences since then, many of which have been confirmed with physical evidence, I can still remember and see and feel that first experience as clear and crystalline as if it were happening right now at this very moment.

Shadowhawk was teaching me about Shamanic journeying when he took me on my first spirit journey or what is also called astral projection or an outer body experience. In the Native American Shamanic tradition drums are used to help the brain reach Alpha brain wave levels, and often rattles and bells are used to push the brain waves deeper into meditative states. In these states the conscious and unconscious mind are easily programmable. Specific emotional reactions and ways of thinking, feeling and behaving can be programmed into the neural networks of the brain very quickly with powerful and lasting results at this level.

In addition, quantum physicists and spiritualists both contend that these techniques of spiritual journeying and astral projection, regardless of the culture they come from are very real and effective means for crossing the boundaries of quantum reality, the various planes of space-time reality.

Shadowhawk began the session with a rhythmic drumming, a four count beat that never varied, tired or faltered. There were seven of us there, students, disciples, learners, all lying down on blankets, the soles of our feet facing each other in a circle, ready to learn the art of spiritual journeying or projection.

At first the experience was similar to other guided mediations I had done, where I imagined or envisioned an experience and went through it. I saw myself visiting my power spot in Horse Thief Canyon, a wild and surprising canyon-land in the prairie of Kansas. And I felt myself running as a coyote but bigger, much bigger, a wolf.

When the journey began, I imagined walking into a cave that slowly transformed into a tunnel. When I eventually came out of the darkness and into the light on the other side, I recognized the canyon's walls and saw the running wolf that I would soon become.

It felt in part like a memory from times before when I had been camping at Horse Thief Canyon. I loved running down the sinuous trails that threaded their way through stands of cottonwood and willow along the stream bottoms and sandstone buttes and grassy hills at the canyon's edges.

Once again, it was like I was running, but this time not in the moccasins I wore back then; instead I was running on heavy, padded and hairy paws. I could feel the sinewy muscles of my canine body and the energy and life coursing through me as I ran, on out of the canyons and across the tall grass prairie.

Then all of a sudden, I heard the drum beat change.

Until it changed, I actually wasn't even aware I was hearing it. Like white noise the constant four count beat Shadowhawk kept had faded into the background. Once the beat changed and quickened however, which was the sign that it was time to return, I became conscious of it and chose to return back to my body. I entered the cave as a wolf and began walking into the darkness.

Soon the darkness swirled and I felt myself re-entering my human body.

The sensation of coming back into my physical form was as real and palpable as any physical, real-world experience I have ever had. I felt my toes push down on the top of my head until a hole opened up, a physical hole like the cranium plates sliding back. And I felt my toes slide down my head, throat and chest, while my hands slid into my fingers like putting on a pair of gloves and my feet slid into my socks like physical things.

I was never the same again.

Once you have had the experience of being embodied or the experience of being disembodied you are never the same again.

After I came back into my body Shadowhawk and I sat talking quietly in the dark for several minutes. "I found my Wolf, I became him. I was running on those sandy trails in the sandstone canyons, out where we collect the gypsum crystals."

"I know Wolf, I was with you, watching you. You did a very good job and found your power spot too."

"You were there? But I never saw you, I never saw any Hawks," I replied.

"That's because I didn't go as a Hawk. I went as one of my other totem animals. Who was running with you out on the prairie?"

"You were the Elk," I exclaimed. In my vision a large bull elk with a massive rack of antlers ran alongside me through the tall prairie grass that spilled out of the mouth of the canyons and stretched on toward the horizon.

"Yes Wolf, this time I was. Remember these visions are real and alive. Everything is real and alive. Keep that in your mind and heart and you will do well."

Then there was the familiar "swoosh" and I found myself plopped right back down in my office chair. My home office has windows that look out across the tiny, tree-filled town of Blue Lake and the beautiful Mad River Valley. My house sits high above the valley on a south facing hill, basking in the sun and it is a very special spatial anchor for me. Several years after my divorce, I realized that I needed to shift where I lived physically in order to complete my emotional shift from resistance and resentment to joyful acceptance and gratitude. And the new house definitely did that for me.

In fact the idea to move was one of those ideas that Corey taught me to call "Inspired Ideas." Inspired Ideas are those absolutely brilliant and bold ideas that just come to you out of nowhere or at least they seem to. In truth, the more aligned you get the more often they come because once you start resonating with the frequency of your true purpose the ideas to bring it about are energetically attracted to you.

For me, as my work with Corey brought me more into alignment with what I truly wanted and what was truly best for me, the idea just popped into my head. I was driving along the dark, curved and icy road that wound around dangerously high river banks and through thick trees to my house, when I saw a flash of sunshine and heard myself say "I am moving to a new house, in the sun."

In the Redwood belt of the Pacific Northwest it rains a lot in the winter, 40 inches a lot, and it is foggy much of the summer, so the sunshine is a valuable and treasured thing. The house that I was living in at the time was very cute, sat on three forested acres right next to a tiny stream and was wonderful in many ways except: it was on the north side of a hill, tucked into a depression, and completely overshadowed by massive redwoods and other trees, so it only saw the direct sunlight for a few hours each day in the late afternoon and thus it kind of depressed me. Not to mention the fact that it was the house I had lived in when I was married. Too many memories, too much past.

So I began intentionally manifesting my new house immediately, as I drove along that dark and icy road. I imagined seeing sunrise and sunset both from the yard. I imagined a rural area, a fantastic view and something similar to my parent's house in Colorado. I knew from my outer-body experiences with Shadohawk and all of my other energy work that thoughts are energy, that like energy attracts like energy and that with enough focus and faith, you can materialize your thoughts, you can manifest your desires, you can bring any idea into physical reality.

Three months later, I was sitting in the living room of my new home, ready to spend my first night in a house that matched my visions to an eerie degree. It even had a cool attic with stairs that dropped down from the ceiling which I had always wanted ever since seeing the movie *Goonies* as a kid.

And as I sat there feeling the feelings of joy and gratitude spin inside me, my MindBody bathing in serotonins, endorphins and other feel-good neuro-chemicals, I felt a shift, much like an earthquake. Except this was just a huge, powerful, single movement, no rocking back and forth, just a single, massive slide and bump, and I realized I was truly and completely grateful for everything that had happened and for my part in manifesting all of it and for what I was going to do with it in the future.

As they say "I felt the love" and it was powerful and real, and it included a love for everything and everyone, even my own mistakes.

Now, every spot in my house, especially those that look out across the valley like my office does, operate as spatial anchors of joy and gratitude for me. It's a nice way to live. I suggest you spatially anchor your home in this way.

A spatial anchor is like a gratitude stone. Whenever you step on that spot, you feel the feelings you have anchored or associated with it. In bullfighting for example, the bull will always return to the same spot in the ring after each pass. This spot is called *La querencia*. It is different for each bull, but each one will pick his own spot and return there, always.

I used to see this same phenomenon in the classes I taught at the University. Even though seats were not assigned, students would assign themselves seats and would always return to the same ones, day after day, after day. And if another student "took their seat" you could tell they were often quite bothered.

So to spatially anchor your home, sit back, relax and take a few deep breaths and say Ahhh, and evoke the emotions you want to feel by recalling times when you felt that way: grateful, joyful, loving, whatever emotions you want to anchor. Notice which way the feelings are spinning inside you and spin them faster and bigger and make the feeling stronger. Then go to that spot in your home and open your eyes and connect your feelings to everything you are seeing, smelling, touching and hearing. And then every time you go to that spot in your home, say a gratitude or think about that feeling and soon it will be automatic and it will happen without you doing anything.

Now every single moment I am at home, I am powerfully reminded, anchored to the certainty that I can manifest anything.

In fact as I grew closer and closer to becoming my full self, I found that the final pieces of the puzzle were falling into place all of their own accord with little to no effort from me, as if the universe were just laying them at my feet.

That is, in fact, how I got my name.

I was alone at Burning Man. A week-long festival, a city of 60,000 people living and partying on a flat desert playa for a week: no cell service, no running water, nothing is sold, everything is given away, no public trash service and no litter, giant sculptures and raging parties on the desert for days, a heady, down the rabbit hole experience for anyone.

Especially if you are alone.

It was my third year and the friend I came with had to leave, so I was alone making temporary friends in a city of 60,000 people, practicing meeting people and having a solo burn of my own. I was walking down 4:00 avenue and two young guys—one in an ostrich costume the other in a pirate outfit—were riding bikes past me and I heard the pirate say "Well, you know, everyone's burn is different, nobody's burn is the same. And that's as it should be."

So I hollered out, "That's so true brother, this year is a totally different burn for me."

And they stopped pedaling and we started talking in common burning man fashion where the assumption is, Not that you are strangers, but that you are Long Lost Brothers of Agreement

And after we discussed our various Burn experiences and how this particular burn was going, in a conversation where I must have emphasized my being alone at the burn, the ostrich turned to me, right before they rode off into the desert night and said:

"Well, you know what they say? You don't always get the burn you want, but you always get the burn you need."

And with that I smiled, looked up to the stars and walked off on my own way alone, to meet my burn, to meet my life, to meet myself and my destiny.

I walked on. In Black Rock City at night when you walk, the playa dust kicks up around your ankles and feet, but you don't notice it like during the day. Your eyes dart, back and forth, transfixed from one neon installation to another, your ears jump and dance, assaulted on all sides by different forms of rave and techno music. When you are alone, the lights and sounds and people guide you. When you are alone, you float around like a moth, flying towards whatever light or sound attracts you.

When you are alone you have no constraints but those you bring with you.

When you are alone you are not even constrained by what other people think of you.

I was very freely alone.

I walked through the dark, toward the light, toward the sound, toward the people.

As it so happened a naming ceremony had spontaneously formed outside of a rave bar and a wide circle of burners, many old veterans some newer and younger, had all assembled and were divining Playa Names for newbies.

You see, in Burner Culture at some point you earn or are given a playa name, which speaks to who you are or something you have done, a name earned in adulthood rather than given during infancy, a powerful and magical name that fits.

So a person without a Playa Name would enter the center of the circle and as we all danced they would tell us their story, tell us about who they were and we would shout out names until we found the one that stuck, the one that both the individual and the group knew was right. I powerfully nailed on my first suggestion for both, the first two people to enter the circle and all eyes turned toward me.

"Who are you," several people asked as we high fived, fist bumped and hugged each other in celebration of finding the most recent name.

"I'm Corey," I shouted over to the core group of burners. Most were dressed in black leather and goggles, hard core and comfortable, steam punk type burner wear for these veterans.

An athletic woman, with muscles rippling up her thighs out of her furry boots and up to her leather bikini and feathered headdress asked "Is that your Playa name? Are you a virgin?"

I explained to the circle that I wasn't a virgin that it was my third year, but I had never gotten a playa name that stuck. So with much hollering and hooting and tequila shooting, they put me in the center of the circle, and with much pomp and circumstance they asked "Who are You? Tell us Your Story?"

In front of me and all around me danced this beautiful little desert nymph with butterfly wings and the stars turned overhead as the music pulsed and beat and the bodies moved, riding the energy of their own emotion, and I said aloud, to the desert sky above the city of 60,000 refugees:

"I am Corey Lewis. I am a life coach and I help people manifest their dreams."

Then as the music pulsed, for one beat all seemed silent until several people all in unison shouted "You are MANIFEST!

As I raised my arms to the sky, I felt the name stick and shouted "I am Manifest," and the crowd of strangers roared, celebrating into the night, celebrating that Manifest was born and that they were there to see it, celebrating the victory of a man they didn't even know.

And after the cheering subsided and the hugs and pats on the back died down, I—Manifest—walked off into the dark desert night alone, to meet others, to make things happen, to Manifest my destiny.

And that's when I leaped without effort or intention it seemed, perhaps I didn't leap but was pushed. In either case, he was there beside me, Corey was there standing with me, the same Corey I was familiar with, a little grayer, a little more muscled, dancing and smiling, a tattoo of tribal lines and fire with the name "Manifest" wrapped around his arm.

"I guess I know what my new tattoo is going to be," I thought to myself.

Because change is the only constant and because we are always experiencing it and because we know on an energetic level that all change is growth, we are our happiest and most fulfilled when we are living on this leading edge, when we are living with a dynamic purpose.

Some of us feel this urge stronger than others and at some times in our lives we feel it stronger than others, but always it is there: An urge to be challenged and to challenge, to grow, learn and overcome, a desire to discover and know and do. This is what makes us uniquely human. This is the drive of our higher nature, the spirit that manifested into physical form.

This is our purpose, your purpose.

To find and live on your own edge.

To find that moment of poise and balance and flow, where you are always pushing and growing, teetering out over the edge to look off in exhilaration and yet not falling over into the abyss, and not retreating from the edge in fear or apathy.

When we are living on this edge is when we feel the most fulfilled. When you look back on your life and find that there are periods that you tell the most stories about that you return to the most often in your memories, these are the periods where you were living on the edge, where you were the most alive.

And generally, these are also not the most comfortable periods of your life either.

If you want to be happy.

If you want to be fulfilled.

If you want your days to be filled with joy and meaning…

Then you must have a purpose.

And the more you believe in and dedicate yourself to that purpose, the more you feel its significance and enjoy its flow, the happier and more fulfilled and successful you will be.

And after you have succeeded, follow the next purpose and attach all your focus, all your energies, on the new goal, in precisely the same way as the last.

Purposes shift. Destinations change. But no one gets anywhere without a goal in mind.

So don't worry about how you will reach your destination and don't avoid starting the journey just because you think you might want to go somewhere else later. Choose a destination, a goal, a dream now, and begin moving toward it. Then later, if you decide on a new destination, you can change your route then and re-navigate on the way, but don't fail to start in the first place.

Don't be afraid to fail. Just begin. Take that first step.

You don't have to be successful to start, but you have to start in order to be successful.

And when one thing ends, move on to something else. When one destination is reached, pick another. When one purpose is fulfilled, find a new one. When one relationship ends, develop a new one to replace it.

It was at this time that Corey gave me a little sneak-peak or preview of my future. Of course I had been badgering him about it all along, especially about whether I would fall in love and marry again, and all he would ever say is: "It's a lot more fun not knowing."

Finally however, he was beginning to loosen up and decided to give me a treat, just one quick leap into my near future.

For this particular leap I started in my office chair, swimming in gratitude and joy, looking out my window at a clear blue sky, across the Mad River toward forested mountains, and I began the countdown. I made note of the silvery energetic cord attaching me to my body as it sat in the chair, and "Three, Two, One" Whooshh, I took off like a rocket soaring up into the bright blue of the sky and on past into widening space, until I crossed the apex of the flight and dropped down through the open doorway that hovered there in space. I fell fast, too fast to see where I was headed and landed with a plop on my butt, in a wooden rocking chair.

One quick look and I knew we weren't at Corey's place in Colorado. We were at my house in Blue Lake and he was sitting right next to me, in my other Adirondack style rocking chair.

"Well, this is interesting." I said. "Why the change of venue? Why here?" Corey never did anything on accident. There was always a specific reason for everything and I had learned it was quickest to just ask him why and get right to it.

He of course was the same way.

"Well C, I like this place." He replied, standing up and walking out on the deck that surrounded the pool.

That pool: it was like the crown jewel for me, the icing on the cake. I had it installed when the boys and I first moved in, cut into the hillside on the south side of the house so it had the same amazing view as my office and was almost part of the house. From my office and from the kitchen and living room, I could look out directly at it and watch the boys swimming and laughing, and from it I could look out across my beloved valley. An expensive item, it also symbolized my certainty of success, the powerful faith and knowing I had that I would be successful in my new career as a coach and author.

"Yeah me too. It means a lot to me, represents a lot to me," I replied.

"It's a good place C. It reminds me of a launch pad for a rocket and not just because it's where you've been launching from these past three years when you come to see me. This is your launch pad C. This is where you are going to start it all from and it is going to be big. Really big. As big as you dream."

"Really? Because I can dream really big," I laughed, "I mean scary big."

"Bigger than that C." Then Corey turned and walked back toward me and we stood facing each other. "We have one more leap to take together. And then there is one more thing I have to tell you C."

Suddenly Corey jumped, launching himself up, sailing straight up into the low hanging ceiling of clouds. I did the same, modeling his movements as best I could: squatting deep and thrusting down hard against the earth, my arms exploding skyward, a head-first dive straight up and into the moist fog.

I felt myself flying, exhilarated with the speed, reveling in the feeling of pure freedom, as I soared up and on out above the clouds. I felt the familiar sensation of slowing down as I reached the apex of my flight and then, the falling momentum of the roller-coaster's drop as I flew back down to whatever time and place Corey had picked for me.

As I dropped down through the gray clouds, unable to see even my hands in front of my face, falling, faster and faster, falling, head over heels, falling, and falling….. I heard Corey's voice in my mind. "Do you remember when you asked me if you would fall in love and have a life-partner again, and I said it was more fun not knowing?"

"Yes," I cried, as I continued falling, faster and faster, falling deeper and deeper.

"I lied," he replied laughing.

And suddenly I found myself sitting in the cockpit of an airplane, flying under a beautiful clear blue sky.

I looked to my right and sitting right next to me, her eyes sparkling and her bright smile beaming at me, was Jessica, my love. And I knew, not only was she my true love for this lifetime, she was also my true love in many lifetimes before and many yet to come. I turned and looked in the cabin behind us and there sitting in the familiar four seats of a Piper Cherokee Six airplane, were my two boys and her two girls, all smiling and talking and quite a bit older than they are now. The familiar feel of our family on vacation, my own plane and my soul-mate beside me, felt thousands of years old and as new as the morning dew on the grass at the same time.

And I knew that Corey had finally taken me to my future.

We smiled to each other and I heard us repeating a phrase that we made up or remembered, in the first few months of our love, a phrase that reminded us how many lives we had led together, and how grateful we were to be together again in this one

"Finally, Again!" We both said in unison.

"Finally, again, we have found each other." We repeated as her eyes crinkled up and smiled and flashed in that oh so special way.

"Finally, Again…"

Then as I looked at her, getting lost in her eyes, I felt the familiar swoosh and leaped again.

This time I found myself in my bedroom in my parent's house in Kansas; it's 1985 and I'm a young teenager sitting on my bed and staring, mesmerized, at the cover of the national geographic. The photo is iconic and many men who saw it fell in love, even you will remember her: the girl with the green eyes, black hair and red shawl. Sharbat Gula, a Pashtun Afghani woman photographed by Steve McCurry. She was exactly the same age as me at this time, and I can remember staring at her for long hours, putting someone like her in my vortex, in my desires, in my future and she looked oh so very much like Jessica.

Then the room spun and blurred and I felt the familiar swoosh of a leap, but without movement this time. It only took me a moment to realize I had leaped to 2014, to what is now my "old" room, and I'm back visiting my parent's.

I have now been quantum leaping for over a year and this book, *The Art of Becoming*, is almost finished. I'm visiting my parents in Topeka, at their little horse farm where I grew up and I'm getting ready for bed in my old bedroom which I shared with Bart. Everything is so familiar, it is like being joyously haunted by the past, like living in nostalgia. I look at the windows and remember how many times we climbed out of them to sneak out at night and run around the neighborhood. I think about how many long hours we laid on the big bed and talked deep into the night about our lives, and the world and what it all meant.

I decide that I want something to read in bed, something different than the nonfiction book I brought with me, something with more of a story, so I find myself standing in front of the bookshelf scanning titles until one hits me: A bright blue spine with three words written in white flowing typeface: Richard Bach *One.*

I open the front cover of the book and read inside this simple inscription, written in my own hand 26 years before: "To Dad, From Corey, Christmas 1988." Suddenly the world swirls and blurs, a sound like wind rushes in my ears, and I find myself standing in the living room of my parents' house with a teenaged Corey standing in front of me. Surrounding us, the entire family is circled up in the living room. A Christmas tree stands in the corner and the floor is littered with bright piles of wrapping paper and presents.

My dad is opening a present and I watch my 16-year-old self talk excitedly to my dad about how much he loves the book. "It's all about Quantum Physics and leaping across time and space to parallel universes and true love Dad, it's awesome!"

In the book, Richard and his soul-mate Leslie are flying along in their Sea Bee plane when suddenly they find themselves quantum jumping from one parallel universe to another. In each new reality they meet a version of themselves and exchange lessons about their lives and choices. In one world, they even come very close to not being together.

I realized when the Universe dropped the book in my lap again that the seeds were planted long ago, that I've known how to do this for many years, that our teachers are everywhere, that we are speaking to ourselves all the time, that I can leap to any self that I want.

And I realized that if there was something I wanted, especially love, I should go for it fearlessly. And that's exactly what I did when I returned to Humboldt. I loved so powerfully and fearlessly and joyfully that no obstacle could get in my way.

I put her in my vortex a long time ago. And I'm with her now and I can see us together in the future. I have come along a full circle of healing. I have become aligned with my higher self and future self. I am manifesting everything I desire faster than ever before.

In a flash the glimpse was gone and I was jerked backward, racing through space and time, until I was dropped right back down in my desk chair at home, facing the Mad River Valley and my glowing computer screen.

Corey stood behind me. I could feel his presence.

"It's over, isn't it?" I said, without turning around.

"Yes it is. You can still come see me if you want, but you don't need to. It's time. It's time for you to Be me C. It's time for you to Become Corey." And with that he stepped forward and stepped right into me.

I felt him merge with me, that old familiar sensation I felt on my first outer body experience with Shadowhawk. Then inside my head I heard his voice, our voice, say with complete certainty.

"I will no longer call you C. You have become fully me."

"Now, I am Corey. I am Manifest. And I'm on Fire!"

I smiled and cried for quite some time. The salty warm tears streamed down my cheeks while I grinned and laughed. With a smile, I looked out across the Mad River Valley, the river high, the water swirling with rain and salmon, and reached for my computer keyboard and began to write:

In the end which is also the beginning, I hope, dear reader, you have already realized that this book, these conversations and stories and strategies will help you to make your life, and the lives of those around you, abundantly better than you used to dare dream.

I know that you can easily have hope and find faith and can feel certainty that everything is already unfolding for you as it should and that you can and will and already are manifesting the results you want.

In the end, I want you to be your own beginning.

I want you to master your mind easily and to get the life you want quickly which you will now that you know and realize the Art of Becoming lies in Being and you are ready to always, already Be who you want to Become.

I wonder how eager you are to experience yourself as the powerful spiritual being you are, now that you can easily and often align with your higher self and enjoy the avalanches of abundance that are now flowing to you and through you for the rest of your days.

TOOLS, TECHNIQUES AND RESOURCES

"So, you remember learning about memory pegs in the Silva Method?" Corey asked me one evening.

"Of course," I quipped laughing, "how could I forget them?" I had been using the Silva Method of memory pegs for years.

As I discussed earlier, Jose Silva founded the Silva Method of Mind Control many years ago. He and Richard Bandler the creative genius behind NLP are, in my opinion, the most influential and important figures in the personal growth, human potential field. In addition to discovering the effectiveness of programming the mind at Alpha brain wave levels, Jose Silva also realized and made use of the mind's ability to think and store information in images. Working with images, whether for programming work or memorization is extremely effective because it uses the right hemisphere of the brain in addition to the left. Thus when we work with images we are activating a greater area of our brain and thus we are thinking at a much higher level, in fact, at a genius level compared to our standard thinking at beta brain wave levels which relies almost exclusively on the left half of the brain alone.

In addition, just as the old adage says, a picture is worth a thousand words. An image in our mind can store a wealth of information. Think for example of a dream you have had. As soon as you see the image, say, of being at someone's house for a party, you already know whose house it is, who else is there, the occasion for the party and a whole host of other detailed contextual information. All of this wealth of detailed information is stored in the image.

We can make use of our brain's ability to store vast amounts of detailed information visually by consciously choosing to use images to memorize information. In the Silva Memory Peg Method, you relax and count yourself down to Alpha level, then you program in images which will become your memory pegs, upon which you will later hang the information you want to remember. The first ten memory pegs in the Silva Method are images that relate to the numbers 1 through 10.

They are as follows: 1. A cup of Tea. 2. Noah the builder of the arc. 3. A calendar opened to the month of May. 4. A ray of sunshine. 5. A Police man. 6. A man or dog with a big Jaw. 7. A key. 8. A fee or price tag. 9. An ocean bay. 10. Toes.

Silva Method Memory Pegs

You could create and program in any image for each number, and you can program in as many memory pegs as you want. These are just ten simple images that I find easy to relate to each number. You don't have to stop at ten.

Once you have the memory pegs memorized or programmed in, they will remain forever in your long-term memory. Then whenever you want to remember specific information, like a list of groceries to buy for example, simply hang each item, visually in your mind on a memory peg. For example, I might imagine a hot dog in my cup of tea, Noah holding charcoal briquettes and hot dog buns pictured on the calendar showing the month of May and so on. Later when I'm at the store, all I need to do in order to remember my list is to visualize each memory peg and the new item will be part of that image reminding me of what it was that I wanted to buy.

Once you have programmed the memory pegs into your long-term memory, you can hang any number of items on them and you will find yourself able to recall them with ease and precision later at any time that you want.

"Well C, I have an updated version of Memory Pegs. It will allow you to push your memory farther. It's gonna blow your mind actually. It's called MindFile." He paused. "So you want to learn it?"

"You bet" I replied, and a few seconds later we were ten thousand miles to the east and two thousand years in the past. I found myself walking down a long hallway with walls and floors of polished marble. From the rooms that adjoined the long hall, I could hear a constant murmur of voices, low and hushed like the soft, continuous flow of a babbling brook

Occasionally I peeked into those rooms and saw in each one, a lone man reciting long lines of verse from memory. Most also carried parchment in their hands and from time to time they would look at it this and then return to their recitations with closed eyes. At different intervals, they each would leave the room they were in, enter another one and repeat the process. As I watched and listened, I began to notice that as a new man entered a room, he recited the same verses as the last person, as if each room was dedicated to a specific set of lines.

Suddenly I realized I was witnessing a long lost part of history. It is well-known that the ancient Greeks had a wide variety and great number of mnemonic or memorizing devices or strategies, most of which have been lost to us over the ages. The thick tome *The Iliad and the Odyssey* for example and the other adventures of Ulysses, were not books in Greek times as they are today. They were memorized poems spoken and sung out loud from memory by Greek bards and represented one of the greatest feats of memorization recorded in human history. Exactly how these bards memorized so much information, recalling hundreds and thousands of lines, word for word, is not known. We do know that they often used repeating stock phrases, such as "the wine dark sea" in order to make memorization easier, but we don't know all of their methods.

One method that we have a brief description of, but which has never been fully known is that somehow these bards would visualize walking through a mansion in their minds and on each wall they would see pages of their memorized text visually and they would then recite their lines by reading them directly off this image. Exactly how the Greeks did this however, has never been discovered by scholars and historians.

Until now, I realized. Suddenly I became aware of what I was witnessing. I was watching this lost piece of history in action.

And then I heard Corey's voice in my ear. "You've seen enough, now come with me."

Suddenly I felt that familiar pulling, whooshing feeling and we were in a dark movie theater, watching Tom Cruise in *Minority Report*. He stood in his pre-crime office using the holo-computer, visually moving files in the air with his hands.

Then I felt a swoosh and a pull and I was standing outside of my own house in Blue Lake California.

"I wanted you to see those scenes C, so you would have some context for where this technique comes from and how it works. MindFile works very similarly to how the Greeks used an image of a many-roomed mansion to store information, but it borrows from our more modern experiences of using computers, file folders and holographic imaging."

"So now C, we are going to set up your MindFile system with this visualization which we are doing together. Later whenever you want to store or retrieve information in your MindFile you can return here on your own through meditation."

We went into the house and walked down the hall and into my bedroom. There on the wall above my bed was a giant holo-computer screen. I could see the tabs of several blank folders already on the screen over on one side. Corey opened one of these tabs by drawing his finger across it just as you would on a touchscreen computer and on it was a picture of a guy's head and you could see, kind of holographically that there were files or file folders arranged in his head. Corey opened one of these files by flipping the image to the left and there on the white page, I began to read the following:

MindFile:

How to Store a Secret or Any Amount of Information

"So, you remember learning about memory pegs in the Silva Method?" Corey asked me one evening.

That's when I stopped reading and turned toward him to ask "Uh, what the...?"

He cut me off, gesturing toward the wall. "This here in this file, this is part of the book *The Art of Becoming*. It is in fact, the entire section you are going to write for the book about learning the MindFile technique. It's all stored here for you, all done. I thought I'd save you some time."

"Thanks Corey, but uh, why don't you explain to me how it works."

"Ok, so anytime you want to store some information especially if it's a lot of information and it has to be remembered precisely this is what you will do.

Visualize walking into your house, down the hallway and into your bedroom. See your room very clearly and write the information you want to remember on the wall or on an imaginary black board on the wall or an imaginary computer screen on the wall. See it clearly on the wall or screen in front of you.

Then turn around and look at each of the other walls in the room and back at the screen wall, and see it and say the information again. Then exit the room once and walk back into the room and see and say your stored information one more time. Then leave the house.

Anytime you want to recall that information, visualize going back into your house, walking into that room and seeing the screen. In fact just for fun, I recommend trying it the next day or every few days to check on your visualization and to practice the technique.

As you succeed your confidence will increase and as your confidence increases your skill will also increase.

For a more advanced version, you can create a filing system on the wall. Each secret or bit of information is in a file that is symbolized by a picture. These could be memory pegs, as in the Silva system or they could relate to the information being stored, like a picture of a combination lock on the file that has a series of pass codes or a picture of your child's or parent's face on the file that contains their birthdate, social security number, phone number, address, medications they are allergic to and so on.

You will follow the same process as before. Visualize entering the house and the room, and see the computer screen on the wall (or stack of pictures). Leave the picture on the wall and open it as if you were opening a book. See and say the information inside. Then turn and look at a different wall in the room and turn back to the file, see the image on the front of it and open it so you can see and say the information. Then leave the bedroom, go into another room and then return to the bedroom, see the picture on the wall, open the file and see and say the information one last time.

Each time you want to create a new file, enter your house, walk into your room and flip through all the pictures that are there on the wall. Flip each picture to the side, until you have gone through them all and then create your new picture and new file. In order to retain all the files you have placed there before, it is helpful to flip through them each time you create a new file.

And remember C, that it will help you when you are visualizing to allow yourself to use your hands and fingers in the air out in front of you just as if you were physically flipping the pages, or using a touch screen on a computer."

As Corey's voice faded out, I felt that familiar swoosh and we were back on his deck sipping tea.

"So when you get back home C, go to Alpha level, visualize going into your house and see your screen. Then open the MindFile folder and you will see this entire section of the book, written verbatim as it appears now, in print."

"Really? The entire section, all of it? Exactly as I'll write it for the final version of the book? How much information can you store in there?"

"Oh the amount is limitless. If you can see it, if you can visualize it then it's there. It will be there when you return. But you have to see it there first. You have to take the time at Alpha level to program it in, to put the writing on the wall so to speak."

"Now I've already done this for you at Alpha level with this section of the book. So you will find in there a set of files under the icon that looks like a toolbox. This is the series of exercises and handouts for the appendix of the book. Come back here, open them, read them and then write them and we will have the appendix finished and the book can be published and it can get out there and start helping people to CHANGE! You know what I mean C?"

"Yeah ok, I will," I replied. "But I don't understand how can it already be stored there, NOW, exactly as it WILL be published in the future? I mean what about revisions and everything?"

"I'll have to explain how that works later, but just know for now C, it's exactly the way it will be published." Then, just before the swhoosh came to send me home, he added, with a wink and a smile "And don't worry about the minor typo, no one will notice."

The principles of using visual images and mental associations to aid in memory enhancement can be applied in other ways as well. For example, if you wanted to remember that same list of items without the memory pegs, you could create a Visual Narrative, a story with pictures of each item associating with, or relating to the others. So for example, you could visualize the hot dogs marching down the street like in a parade, the buns opening and closing on them like cymbals, the charcoal following behind like a large float, the cups and plates rolling along and so on.

Then when you are in the store, you just re-tell yourself the story in its same familiar order and the images will reappear in your mind, telling you what to buy.

Other principles that aid in learning and memorization that you will keep in mind as you study these strategies and practice these techniques are:

First, put things into groups of 3 or 4. The mind remembers best in small groups like this; that's why phone numbers and credit card numbers are divided as they are. So for spelling, for example, split the word up into 3 to 4 letter groups; regardless of the subject, cluster groups in this way. And remember to visualize, spelling is best done visually like most forms of memorization, especially because you can't "sound out the words" in a language like ours that is not phonetic (hell, even the word "phonetic" isn't fonetik).

Second, repetition of studying and self-testing is best for memorization, so study one group, self-test and study again, until it's memorized then move on to the next group. And after you self-test, simply study and memorize the items you didn't get correct on the self-test, until you have them all.

Third, we grow new cortical pathways at night when we sleep, so study over multiple days and go to Alpha level each time before you study.

Fourth, using more than one sense when studying such as saying it out loud to engage the auditory sense and writing it down to engage the kinesthetic sense helps us remember better because it adds at least one more of our five senses in association with the remembered information.

Finally, and most importantly Dr. Bandler would say that you learn best when your brain is flooded with endorphins and serotonin, when you are happy, confident, curious and interested. So while you practice and learn, remember we aren't doing this for grades but for good times, these aren't serious lessons they are fun learnings, there's no failure only feedback, no dunces only development.

So, let the games begin...

How to Use this Appendix

In order to maximize your mind, in order to optimize your mental and physical potential you need to exercise your mind:

Stretch it to make it more flexible, creative and open, so it has more choices, possibilities and potential solutions.

And strengthen it so that it thinks and learns faster, remembers longer and more accurately and processes more intelligently, intuitively and rationally.

If you do this, you will feel better and perform better in every situation and thus you will get better results back from life, which will in turn yield better feelings and even better behavior and even better results and so on. And while those better results are adding up, you will continue to use these methods to optimize your MindBody and those benefits will compound like interest on an excellent investment until you are enjoying avalanches of abundance in every category of life.

It is vitally important to leverage this power of compounding in your favor. You see, in much the same way that interest is compounded on an investment and then more interest is paid on that interest, if we continue the process of optimization and self-improvement, after we start getting better results from life we will compound benefits upon benefits.

Imagine for example, that we were going to play 18 holes of golf and bet 10 cents per hole. Now that wouldn't amount to much money, so even if you were a terrible golfer you might take the bet. At worst, you could only lose $1.80, not much to worry about.

However, what if I said let's double the bet each hole. That still doesn't seem like it would amount to much. I mean after all, how much could it really amount to? After all it's only ten cents, right?

Well, if you do the math it gets quite interesting because of the power of compounding. The first few holes aren't that surprising: after hole #1, you owe me 10 cents, then 20, then 40 and by hole #4 it's 80 cents. Not much to worry about.

But things start adding up pretty fast when we get to the later holes. By hole #12 you owe me $204.80 and by hole #15 that figure has jumped to $1,638.40. Now you are starting to get worried. And by hole #18 it has grown to the astronomical figure of $13,107.20. All from a 10 cent bet.

Now that is the power of compounding.

When you start doing these exercises and things improve and then you continue doing them and things improve more and then you persist and keep continuing to do them, then things will improve even more and more and opportunities and successes will compound on each other again and again and again… And again!

And in order to get all that good stuff, you have to, you get to, you will do the work.

It works, if you work it. It doesn't, if you don't.

And you will.

Say this out loud: "I will."

Say this out loud: "I am."

Quantum Leaping to Your Future Self

When you listen to the recorded trance induction accompanying this book or when clients work with me in person, I use a variety of hypnotic techniques, language patterns and guided meditation imagery to lead you through the quantum leaping process. In the absence of either of those tools, this resource in the appendix is a description for how to get yourself down to Alpha brain wave levels and how to visualize quantum leaping to your future self on your own.

Read this several times so that you can repeat the steps from memory then engage in the process and have fun.

1. Make sure you won't be disturbed by people, phones or other intrusions for 30 minutes to 1 hour. Find a comfortable chair to sit in, perhaps with a head rest and a slight decline, but do not lay down or recline too fully or you may go to sleep. Begin relaxing by closing your eyes and taking a few deep breaths, in and out, and on one of those breaths let out an audible "Aaaahhhh" of relaxation and contentment.

    Set your intention for what self or doppelganger you want to go meet. Is it yourself 10 or 20 or 40 years into the future so that you can learn from your more experienced wisdom? Or is it your past self of 10 or 20 or 40 years ago so you can give yourself the resources and understandings and comfort you needed then? Or is it a different self, one that you feel you cannot become on this plane from another plane of the multi-verse? No matter which self you want to connect to, make a clear intention to go to them, evoke the feeling of them and some idea of who that self is before you leap.

    This is called *Setting the Intention.*

2. When you begin to talk to yourself in order to relax yourself down into Alpha, use a sleepy, relaxed, calm voice. It even helps to yawn in your mind and to call up relaxing, calming, sleepy feelings.

   Start by saying or paraphrasing the following: "I am deeply relaxed and relaxing further. I can feel a raindrop of relaxation dropping on my head and washing all over me from head to toe, relaxing and warming and loosening each muscle along the way. I can feel the muscles of my scalp and face relax and loosen as the relaxation washes down my body. I can feel the muscles of my face and neck relax and loosen as my eyelids and head get heavy. And the relaxation washes down further making the muscles of....."

   Then continue with this process all the way to your toes so that you have focused on and physically relaxed each and every part of your body.

   This is called *The Head to Toe Relax.*

3. Next, to deepen your relaxation further and drop deeply down into Alpha brain wave levels, say or paraphrase to yourself the following:

   "I'm going to count down from 10 to 1, and each number is going to double my relaxation, until I am in Alpha state." Then you will say each number three times and visualize it directly in front of you, filling up your field of vision: "Ten, Ten, Ten" you will say, while you see "10, 10, 10" or some version of that. Then you will say "My relaxation has doubled and I am dropping down into Alpha, I am in Alpha now. Nine, Nine, Nine" and so on, until you say and see "1, 1, 1."

This is called ***The Ten to One Countdown.***

4. Now, visualize and feel yourself floating out of your body and up into the sky. Look back and notice that there is a long and strong silvery cord connecting you to your body, so that you can always return to the here-now from any time-space you want. Visualize yourself floating onward, upward through the clouds, on out into space, far, far, above the earth, until you are in the deep, airless regions of space above our orbiting globe. As you feel your speed slow and the trajectory of your arc flatten out, you know you are reaching its zenith, its apex, the peak.

    Everything slows down and as your velocity pauses, you see a doorway before you. Watch your hand reach out and open it and feel yourself step through and begin to lean forward into your downward descent as you begin to fall rapidly, in a fast, free-falling, sky-diving like flight back toward the spinning planet below you. Visualize and feel yourself dropping down into…. Whatever images swirl and come up in front of you as you land on earth near or inside yourself, get ready to watch and learn from yourself like never before.

    When you visit your doppelganger watch what your other self does, feel how your other self feels, note how they talk and don't worry if you don't understand what they say or what you see. In time, you will come to figure out, interpret and understand your experience if it is not already immediately clear to you.

    This is called ***Making the Leap.***

5. Spend some time with your other self, with your doppelganger. Do whatever feels natural.

You might have a conversation with them. Start by asking them questions about themselves, about things you want to know and learn. And wait and listen and watch and feel for their answers. Some might come in unexpected ways. You might also want to follow them around and watch what they do, how they move, what they say to others, what their daily life is like.

At times you may want to "associate" with them or become them. In order to do this, step inside them so that you are looking out of their eyes and seeing and doing and feeling things from their perspective. Take your time and absorb their presence, their energy, their unique vibration.

This is called *Taking it In.*

6.   Return on the same path you came. Follow the silver cord if you need to or just set the intention to leap back, or your other self will often just thrust you back.

Once you are back in your body, if you are powerfully inspired to immediately write, paint, build or do something, then by all means immediately go do it. Leave the dishes in the sink, the emails un-answered, the dog unfed and go get it done.

On the other hand, if when you come back you feel a powerful heady feeling, like you are ready to pounce but there is a lot to process, then relax for a few minutes with your eyes open. Now it is time to begin writing down everything you saw, felt, heard and did. Jot down your immediate recollections, even if they don't make sense. Take as many notes as possible. What did your doppelganger look like, say, do? Where was he or she? How did you feel? How did they feel? What were they wearing, what items did you see around them? In time these details will come to make sense to you, even if they aren't completely understandable when you first write them down.

This is called ***Bringing It Back.***

7. After you have taken a few quantum leaps and begun to make sense of your experiences and notes, clarify what actions they suggest you take. And then take them. Enact them.

Don't worry about whether it makes sense or will lead to success, just do it. Follow your intuition, your spirit guide and keep at it, diligently and persistently until you see results or until your doppelganger corrects your course of action. For example, if the only message you get from your doppelganger is a clear statement that "you should get into sales" and you have no idea what that means or how to do it, then you should simply find any way to follow the suggestion: You might read a bunch of books on sales strategies, attend a sales seminar and so on. These might teach you sales strategies that you will use later on or they might introduce you to the salesman who is going to hire you, depending on your relative profession to manage his company or build her new headquarters or work as his new custodian or whatever.

You never know what will come of taking action, but you always know what happens when you don't take action: Nothing.

This final strategy is called ***Acting It Out.***

217

Daily Power Habits: Seven Strategies for Success

These Daily Power Habits are designed to for alignment and success. They should be practiced faithfully in writing, each morning, for a minimum of 40 days.

After this initial alignment period, you can begin to experiment with how and when you do them each day and you might become more flexible in how you allow yourself to perform them. Regardless, these are habits that we incorporate into our daily life permanently.

While the specific techniques and strategies listed in this appendix for getting over negative feelings or achieving a goal, for example, are extremely helpful in dealing with a specific situation, the Daily Power Habits for Success are geared toward squeezing every bit of joy and possibility and success out of each and every day and situation possible. As you practice these, you will find that old problems like fears, limiting beliefs, bad habits and negative emotional responses begin to dissolve and disappear.

If you read, understand and faithfully practice only one technique in this book, it should be this one. It will pay off in millions of dollars and thousands of joyful days and wonderful moments over your life-time.

Our thoughts become our words. Our words become our deeds.
Our deeds become our habits. Our habits become our Character.
And our character becomes our Destiny.

Required Seven Daily Success Habits for 40 Days and Beyond

1. Incantation

Create an Incantation, Mantra, Affirmation or Spell that you will repeat each day. This incantation should be a powerful and positive statement about who you are, what your purpose is in life and about what you are going to be, do and have without limits. Each day repeat your Incantation 10 times with total emotion, either in front of the mirror or with your chosen power move, pose or power stance.

2. Gratitudes and Powerful Questions

Each Day, Write down 10 things you are grateful for in your life. They can be things that already exist that you appreciate or things that have not happened yet, that you want to happen. Write them out in this way: "I am so grateful for _____ in my life," or "I am so grateful that ____ has happened." Even if it has not happened yet, write it down as if it already has occurred. Remember that what you appreciate appreciates.

In addition, write down 5 Powerful Questions framed in a positive manner. These questions can be about a problem you are having, or some event coming up or any situation you are encountering in life. Write them out in this manner, "What is the best I can imagine _____ going?" Or "What is the best thing I can imagine happening with _____?" "What is the quickest and easiest I can imagine doing _____?" "What is the most fun and success I can imagine having with _____?

Or you might ask, "What is the quickest and easiest and most completely that I can apply the teachings in this book to my life and how radically will I, and my life change for the better until I'm living the life of my greatest dreams and living in abundant joy?"

3. Journaling

Write for a few minutes each day about what you are thinking and feeling, significant experiences you had, insights or goals and dreams or aspirations that you have. You can record what you are thinking and feeling at a given time or in regard to a particular situation, or record questions for your coach if you have one and so on. You can write about dreams and future plans, breakdown and brainstorm future projects, whatever seems useful to you at the time.

4. Meditation

Do at least 15 minutes of meditation, prayer or visual motor rehearsal with relaxed, deep breathing each day. For our purposes meditation is defined as breathing in a relaxed manner, with your eyes closed while remaining awake.

Generally it is best to sit up in a comfortable chair or sitting position. Close your eyes, breathe deeply and relax yourself into Alpha state. You may find that you need to use The Head to Toe Relax and The Ten to One Countdown methods in order to do this at first. Over time you will be able to achieve Alpha much more easily and quickly.

In your meditation you can relax and let your mind empty or you can use visual motor rehearsal to visually rehearse in your mind some future event and see it going wonderfully. You may also use this time to meet with spirit teachers to ask questions for guidance, or you can call up positive feelings and resourceful states by thinking of things you are grateful for and that make you happy and confident and so on.

5. Exercise

Exercise for 30-90 minutes each day in any form that elevates your heart rate. If we maintain our target heart rate for 30 minutes we do much more than burn calories and improve our cardiovascular health (both of which are great). Our metabolism remains boosted for over 24 hours after exercising this long, thus if we exercise every day, we permanently boost our metabolism so that it is higher even when we are not exercising, even when we are sleeping.

We also burn off the stress hormone cortisol when we exercise and release positive neuro-transmitters like endorphins and dopamine which make us happy and motivated. So exercising regularly not only improves your physical health, it also radically improves your emotional health.

For our purposes, exercise is defined simply as any activity that maintains our target heart rate for over 30 minutes: walking, jogging, weight lifting, yoga, martial arts, swimming, surfing, bicycling, mowing the lawn, dancing or any other similar activity can count as your daily dose of exercise.

6. Alkalize

Alkalizing has a variety of benefits that range from fighting cancer and muscle and organ degeneration, to increasing the energetic conductivity of your body which aids in spiritual and emotional alignment.

Alkalize at least once each day with any effective method that you like. A few options for alkalizing are: Drink a few tablespoons of raw organic apple cider vinegar in a full glass of water (I like to add some lemon to it). Or drink kombucha or freshly juiced raw greens such as wheat grass. I prefer to alkalize in the morning before I drink or eat anything else.

And make sure to drink at least 1.5-2 liters of clean, high quality water each day. Most people are partially dehydrated most of the time and the physical, psychological and spiritual effects of this dehydration are significant, causing fatigue, negative emotions and reducing the electrical conductivity, or ki generation and flow of the body.

7. Goal and Task List

Consistently keep a list of Tasks you need to accomplish on a daily or weekly basis, and each day revisit and revise or rewrite this list and check tasks off as you accomplish them.

Find out your own method that works for you. This may include getting and using some form of day-planner, calendar or app for your phone, or writing them down on paper. Regardless, you should have a consistent practice of writing out what needs to be done and when it needs to be done by, and then doing it.

In addition, in your journal begin making a larger list of goals to accomplish in the next few months and years, and the steps need to accomplish them.

The act of writing these tasks down pre-paves you psychologically to complete them and it keeps you organized and moving forward, consistently each day.

Believing in and Achieving a Goal

The primary reason people don't dream big enough or limit themselves when thinking about what they want to do, be and have, is that they don't believe it's possible. They don't believe that their dream, whatever it might be, is possible for them.

And if they do dare to admit to themselves what they truly want, they rarely achieve it for the same reason: they don't truly believe it is possible.

In order to achieve any goal, first you have to believe it is possible for you. Then you have to build the emotional investment required to motivate yourself and build the necessary propulsion system required to drive you there.

Once you have clearly defined *What* you want and connected fully to *Why* you want it, the *How* will take care of itself.

These steps will help you with that process.

1. Define your goal in terms of what you want (not what you don't want). Make sure to write your goal out in positive statements and terms.

    Then write down all the positive benefits of getting or accomplishing it. These should include everything from the direct benefits to indirect and cascading benefits like you feeling better about yourself and more confident because you will have proven to yourself you can do anything you put your mind to.

    Then write down all the negative consequences of not getting or accomplishing your goal, again including indirect consequences such as making you question your abilities and lose your self-confidence.

This step will instill in you the psychological investment to take action. It will fuel you up emotionally to put you into motion.

2. Write down all the reasons that you know you will succeed and those people and things that support you. Include past things you have succeeded at, others who have succeeded at your goal, skills and resources you have or have access to and anything else that supports your success.

   This step will help you to believe so you can achieve. It will convince you that your dream or goal is possible for you.

3. Write down 3-5 powerful and positive questions each day: questions framed in a positive way, asking about the "best" or "most success" possible with your goal.

   For example, "What is the quickest, easiest and most fun I could imagine having while accomplishing my goal?" Or, "What is the most amount of fast and effective and productive progress I can imagine making toward my goal today?"

   This step will open you and the universe up to finding the best and most effective solutions to your problems and possibilities for your success.

4. Write down 5-10 gratitudes every day related to your goal, the process of achieving it and how you will feel once you have accomplished it.

Write them out as if the goal has already been accomplished. For example, "I am so happy and grateful now that I have done _____."

This step will help you gain confidence and gratitude in taking the steps along the way toward your goal and will help you increase what you are grateful for because what you appreciate appreciates.

5. Write down an affirmation that states in positive terms that you will accomplish your goal or that you already have and repeat it 3-5 times each with strong emotion.

    For example, you might write something like, "I am so happy and grateful now that I have accomplished _____ in my life and now that I am doing _____ and have _____. I am _____ and I can and will do _____."

    This step will connect your confidence in achieving your goal to your own self-identity and makes use energetically of the most powerful statement in the English language: I am.

6. Create a vision card or poster that you can look at every day that contains images related to your goal or images of you already having accomplished it.

    You can cut these pictures out of a magazine, download them off the internet or whatever you like. You can also write on the card or poster what your goal is. The images and words on the poster should make you feel wonderful about and attracted to your goal while making you want to take steps toward achieving it. Look at this poster several times each day.

This step will connect you to your goal visually and help you manifest it into physical form from your imagination. Because everything that exists was imagined first.

7. Use The Head to Toe Relax and The Ten to One Countdown to go to Alpha state and then imaginatively rehearse or see, yourself going through the steps required to achieve your goal and see yourself succeeding at your goal on a daily basis.

    See, hear and feel how it will feel to succeed at accomplishing each step toward your goal and the final accomplishing of your goal, and enjoy it until it feels like you have already done it!

    This step of visual motor rehearsal will pre-pave you to successfully take each step toward your goal, making each physical effort easier and more effective.

8. When you are feeling aligned, inspired or empowered to work on your goal, brainstorm steps, ways, options, tasks, intermediary goals and benchmarks to accomplish on the way to your main goal.

    Write out answers to these questions, "where am I now in relationship to my goal?" "what are some of the steps I will have to take along the way?" "what is the first step I can take and what is the deadline by when I will take it?" "what is the second step I can take and what is the deadline by when I will take it?"

    This step, working on your goal when you are energetically aligned with it, will put you into the "flow-state" where your work is effortless, playful and amazingly effective.

9. Create "To Do" lists every day or every week to focus on the next steps or tasks for achieving your goal and cross off each item on the list as you accomplish it.

   Make a consistent habit of accomplishing one task each day or several tasks each week and celebrate the completion of each step as you cross it off your list. And really celebrate when you reach important benchmarks so that you make the process of working on your goal, fun and playful.

   This step will help you build momentum as you move toward your goal so that you can blow right through the obstacles and resistances you will encounter along the way.

10. Use an accountability partner or partners to keep you working consistently toward your goal.

    This is a person or a small group of people who you are close to and have told about your goal, someone who supports you in achieving it and wants you to win. Ask this person to check in with you once each week to ask you about your progress and hold you accountable for inaction and to celebrate successful action.

    This step will support you as you work to manifest your goal and it will make it more physically real to you as you share out loud with others your desire.

How to Clear Negative Emotions

(Loss, Anger, Fear, etc.)

Negative emotions always stem from resistance, from our refusal to accept or embrace external circumstances as they are. And in addition to making us feel bad in the moment, they reduce our ability to take effective action making us feel bad later as well.

In fact, if you reflect back on your life you will see that every bad choice or decision you made was made when you were in a negative emotional state, and every good choice or decision was made when you were in a positive state or feeling good.

Feelings of loss, regardless of the source, are about an attachment to the past and a refusal to embrace the present.

Feelings of anger, regardless of the source, are about an attachment to what we think the present "should" be and a refusal to embrace it as it is.

And feelings of fear, regardless of the source, are about a resistance to potential futures that may or may not ever occur.

So in summary, loss is about the past, anger about the present and fear about the future.

The methods for clearing them are the same, because each negative feeling is simply a form of resistance and once we clear our resistance the feeling goes away.

Write out the following and be as specific as you can:

"I create the experience of _____ (fill in the negative emotion or

belief here) Because my

Past Programming Demands that _____ (fill in the demand

or cause here)."

Here are three potential examples:

1. I create the experience of loneliness and unhappiness (loss) because my past programming demands that I be in a relationship to be happy.
2. I create the experience of frustration and impatience (anger) because my past programming demands that kids do what parents say immediately.
3. I create the experience of stress and anxiety (fear) because my past programming demands that I believe that things will be difficult and will probably go wrong and I should constantly think about them as if they really are going to happen in order to avoid them.

Once you write it out this way you will see how un-realistic and unhealthy and changeable that demand or belief is. Simply identifying the past programming that is causing the negative feeling will weaken it without any other work.

Next, to remove the negative programming completely, turn the demand into a preference:

1. "I prefer to be in a relationship but I'm happy without one."
2. "I prefer that kids listen and obey easily but I understand they are children and sometimes won't."

3. "I prefer that things work out easily and don't go wrong, but I can easily solve any difficulties or problems that arise.

Then write out repeatedly the opposite of the demand:

1. "I am happy not being in a relationship."
2. "I am happy when kids don't listen right away."
3. "I am happy when problems arise and need to be solved."

Finally, write 3-5 gratitudes or positive re-phrasings of the demand each day:

1. "I am happy not being in a relationship right now." "I am grateful that there is space in my life for me to find a truly fitting partner." "I'm am happier being with myself than with the wrong person for me."
2. "I am grateful that I have learned patience and to see the humor in kid's behavior." "I am happy that their behavior calls on the best part of me as a teacher or parent to respond." "I am happy I have this opportunity to help them learn and grow."
3. "I am grateful that everything is going to work out well and I will feel good the whole time until it's all over." "I am grateful when difficulties arise and I have a chance to grow and become better." "I am grateful that everything is okay right now and I can keep a positive frame of mind about the future."

Use The Head to Toe Relax and The Ten to One Countdown to reach Alpha state and create an image of yourself in relation to the negative feeling or belief (or of the person you harmed or who harmed you if there is someone involved in the negative feeling or belief). Perhaps this will be a memory of a past experience or something you imagine or fear might happen.

Hold that image in your mind clearly and repeat as many times as you want, the following four phrases. Say them to the image of yourself. (If applicable, say them to the image of whoever you hurt, or imagine whoever hurt you saying them to you.) Say them repeatedly.

These are the only four things we ever need to hear whenever we are hurt or have hurt. They heal all wounds. This comes from an ancient Hawaiian healing technique passed down among the Kahunas and is called Ho'oponopono. It is explained in detail in Joe Vitale's wonderful book *Zero Limits* where he describes many of the amazing therapeutic cures Hawaiian psychologists and healers have achieved with the technique.

Repeatedly say:

I am sorry
Please forgive me
Thank you.
I love you.

Next, imagine grabbing the image of the negative experience or issue like you would a photograph and wadding it up into a small ball of paper. Then throw that ball of paper as hard as you can and watch it fly out and disappear into the farthest reaches of the universe.

Now, feel inside yourself and find where you are carrying those negative feelings around. Are they in your belly, your back or neck? Find them and imagine reaching into yourself with your hands and pulling them out like pieces of string, or dirt that you are scooping and pulling out. Wad this negative energy up into a ball and throw it to the end of the universe just like you did with the negative picture.

Next, imagine that situation going completely differently. Imagine it exactly as you would like it to be. Make the images big and bright and pull them in close to you. Turn the sounds up nice and loud and step into the image and step into yourself in the image so that you are really there. Now call up the good feelings you would have if it was really that way and you were really there, and spin those feelings larger and faster until you are feeling really good about the situation from your head to your toes.

Do this daily until you shift internally and then your external circumstances will also shift.

ABOUT THE AUTHOR

MindBody Master Dr. Corey Lewis is founder of MindBody Mastery Personal and Professional Development Coaching. He is a Licensed Master Practitioner of Neuro-Linguistic Programming and Neuro-Hypnotic Repatterning who continues to work and train with Dr. Richard Bandler, the Co-developer of NLP. He is also a certified graduate of the Silva Method Meditation system, holds a Ph.D. and is a former University Professor, with a specialty in transformative education.

As a successful business owner and entrepreneur Dr. Lewis has established several businesses and NGO's himself and has helped a number of clients to begin and grow their own businesses. He also has decades of experience working with Non-Profit organizations, managerial teams and sales staff to improve professional performance.

As an athlete, Master Lewis holds a 7th Dan Black Belt in Tae Kwon Do and is a former national champion and Olympic level competitor. He is a Reiki practitioner as well and first began biofeedback training when he was only 11 at the World Famous Menninger Foundation. With his lifelong background in competitive athletics, Master Lewis has coached athletes of every caliber, from amateurs to professionals, on how to improve their performance, pull out of a slump or rise to a new challenge with the most effective an up-to-date methods for psychological and physiological optimization.

Corey combines this lifetime of experience and wide range of skills to help each client find their own best path toward success, and is dedicated to healing the planet by healing the person, one powerful conversation at a time.

For Personal Coaching, Interviews, Speaking Events and Training Seminars with MindBody Master Dr. Corey Lee Lewis

Please contact us with any of the following methods:

1. Quantum leap into any time-space of my experience and say "Hi" with a smile.

2. Physically move into my current time-space at any event, seminar, lecture or reading and say hello with a smile.

3. Visit www.MindBodyMasteryCoaching.com or www.TheArtofBecomingBook.com with a smile.
    [https: mbm coach . com — 2021 UPDATE]

4. Email me at CoreyLewisCoaching@gmail.com with a smile.

5. Write me at Corey, PO Box 1332, Blue Lake, CA, 95525 with a smile.

For helpful articles, videos, information on upcoming seminars and other free content, visit www.MindBodyMasteryCoaching.com sign up for our online newsletter and visit our store.

BIBLIOGRAPHY

Bach, Richard. *Illusions.* Random House. New York, 1977.

---. *One.* Dell Publishing. New York, 1998.

Bandler, Richard. *Richard Bandler's Guide to Trance Formation.* Health Communications Inc., Deerfield Beach. 2008.

---. *Time for a Change.* Meta Publications Inc., Capitola. 1993.

---. *The Secrets of Being Happy.* IM Press. New York, 2011.

Byrne, Rhonda. *The Secret.* Atria Books. New York, 2006.

Emoto, Masaru. *The Hidden Messages in Water.* Beyond Words Publishing. Hillsboro, 2004.

Hicks, Esther and Jerry. *The Law of Attraction.* Hay House. New York, 2006.

---. *Getting Into the Vortex.* Hay House. New York, 2010.

Hill, Napoleon. *Think and Grow Rich.* Penguin Books, 2003.

Sahn Nim, Seung. *Dropping Ashes on the Buddha.* Grove Press. New York, 1976.

Silva, Jose. *The Silva Mind Control Method.* Simon & Schuster. New York, 1977.

Talbot, Michael. *The Holographic Universe.* Harper Perennial. New York, 1992.

Vitale, Joe. *Zero Limits.* John Wiley & Sons Inc. Hoboken, 2007.

Walsch, Neale. *Communion with God.* Berkeley Books. New York, 2000.

Made in the USA
San Bernardino, CA
29 November 2019